W9-BNR-652

The
5-Minute
BIBLE
STUDY
for
Difficult
Times

© 2019 by Barbour Publishing, Inc.

ISBN 978-1-68322-947-6

All rights reserved. No part of this publication may be reproduced or transmitted for commercial purposes, except for brief quotations in printed reviews, without written permission of the publisher.

Churches and other noncommercial interests may reproduce portions of this book without the express written permission of Barbour Publishing, provided that the text does not exceed 500 words or 5 percent of the entire book, whichever is less, and that the text is not material quoted from another publisher. When reproducing text from this book, include the following credit line: "From *The 5-Minute Bible Study for Difficult Times*, published by Barbour Publishing, Inc. Used by permission."

Scripture quotations marked niv are taken from the Holy Bible, New International Version®. niv®. Copyright © 1973, 1978, 1984, 2011 by Biblica, Inc.™ Used by permission. All rights reserved worldwide.

Scripture quotations marked nlt are taken from the *Holy Bible*. New Living Translation copyright© 1996, 2004, 2015 by Tyndale House Foundation. Used by permission of Tyndale House Publishers, Inc. Carol Stream, Illinois 60188. All rights reserved.

Scripture quotations marked kjv are taken from the King James Version of the Bible.

Scripture quotations marked msg are from *THE MESSAGE*. Copyright © by Eugene H. Peterson 1993, 1994, 1995, 1996, 2000, 2001, 2002. Used by permission of NavPress Publishing Group.

Scripture quotations marked nasb are taken from the New American Standard Bible, © 1960, 1962, 1963, 1968, 1971, 1972, 1973, 1975, 1977, 1995 by The Lockman Foundation. Used by permission.

Published by Barbour Books, an imprint of Barbour Publishing, Inc., 1810 Barbour Drive, Uhrichsville, Ohio 44683, www.barbourbooks.com

Our mission is to inspire the world with the life-changing message of the Bible.

Member of the
Evangelical Christian
Publishers Association

Printed in the United States of America.

The
5-Minute
BIBLE
STUDY
for
Difficult
Times

Rae Simons

BARBOUR BOOKS
An Imprint of Barbour Publishing, Inc.

INTRODUCTION

Making regular time to read the Bible can be a challenge in the midst of our busy lives. We resolve to spend a daily hour with the Word, and we start out strong and determined. Soon, though, the demands on our time are so great that our hour with God's Word quickly shrinks to a half hour, then fifteen minutes. . . and then we feel so guilty that we try not to even think about it! Nowhere, though, does God say He requires from us a certain number of minutes. He understands the demands of our daily lives. He doesn't want to punish us— He wants to help us!

This book provides an opportunity for you to spend time regularly with God, reading His Word and responding to Him in prayer—even if you only have five minutes. The book is laid out like this:

Minutes 1–2: **Read** carefully the scripture passage for each day's Bible study.
Minute 3: **Understand.** Ponder two or three prompts designed to help you apply the verses from the Bible to your own life. In spare moments throughout your day, while you're

driving, waiting in line at the grocery store, or doing some mindless task, come back to these thoughts and dwell on them more fully.

Minute 4: **Apply.** Read a brief devotion based on the day's scripture. Think about what you are learning and how to apply the scriptural truths to your own life.

Minute 5: **Pray.** A prayer starter will help you to begin a time of conversation with God. Remember to allow time for Him to speak into your heart as well.

Each selection focuses on a different situation, covering a wide range of difficult experiences and circumstances. As a result, it's not a book that's intended to be read from front to back, in any sort of order. Instead, each time you pick it up, turn to whatever selection seems the best fit with whatever challenge you're experiencing at that moment.

Whether it's those quiet early-morning moments before the rest of your household is awake or the last thing you do before you turn off the light at night, make time for God's Word to enter your life. You may be surprised by the difference just five minutes can make!

I DON'T KNOW WHAT TO PRAY

READ ROMANS 8:22–28

KEY VERSE:
We do not know what we ought to pray for,
but the Spirit himself intercedes for
us through wordless groans.
ROMANS 8:26 NIV

UNDERSTAND:
- What does the phrase "wordless groans" say to you? Is it a good description of how you feel when you don't know how or what to pray? Why or why not?
- Notice that this Bible passage uses the same word—*groan*—to describe both the Holy Spirit's intercession and the state of all creation as it waits for the birth of something new. What do you think this implies?

APPLY:
In childbirth, a woman moves past the ability to talk in coherent words. The process of delivery is so intense that every morsel of her being— mental, emotional, and physical—is completely

focused on this amazing act that breaks her open in order to bring new life into the world.

In this passage of Paul's letter to the Romans, he compared our current state of reality to that intense process of birthing a baby. We cannot control our circumstances, any more than a woman can control childbirth. With that in mind, we don't *need* to know what to pray. After all, we can't tell God what needs to happen, and He doesn't need us to tell Him. Instead, we can simply surrender to the Spirit. God is with us in this process. He feels the same pain we do, and He will pray through us, birthing His Spirit into our hearts and the world around us.

PRAY:
Loving Lord of life, I don't know how or what to pray—so I ask that You pray through me. I surrender myself to Your Spirit. Be born in me.

I'M OVERWHELMED BY MY RESPONSIBILITIES

READ 2 CORINTHIANS 1:8–10

KEY VERSE:
We were crushed and overwhelmed beyond our ability to endure, and we thought we would never live through it. . . . But as a result, we stopped relying on ourselves and learned to rely only on God.
2 CORINTHIANS 1:8–9 NLT

UNDERSTAND:
- Even the apostle Paul, the great hero of our faith, went through times when he felt life was asking more of him than he could handle.
- As Paul pointed out, if God can raise the dead to life, He can certainly also handle the demands of our daily lives!

APPLY:
Although we may never be called to endure all that the apostle Paul did in his service to God, we all have times when our lives overwhelm us. Our to-do lists just keep getting longer; no

matter how hard we try, we can't seem to catch up. We may not think we're going to actually die from the pressure, as Paul did, but we do feel frustrated and hopeless and discouraged. We may blame others for putting these demands on us—or we may blame ourselves for not being able to accomplish more.

But Paul said there's a solution to this problem: Stop trying to do so much in our own strength! Day by day, put it all in God's hands. He will accomplish through us what He needs us to do—and whatever remains undone, we can trust Him to handle.

PRAY:
God, You know how busy I am. I'm exhausted from the effort of trying to keep up with everything. I don't know how much longer I can go on like this, so I'm giving it all to You. Accomplish through me whatever needs doing—and I'll leave whatever's still undone in Your hands.

MY LIFE SEEMS SO BORING

READ EPHESIANS 3:14–21

KEY VERSE:

And I ask him that with both feet planted firmly on love, you'll be able to take in with all followers of Jesus the extravagant dimensions of Christ's love. Reach out and experience the breadth! Test its length! Plumb the depths! Rise to the heights! Live full lives, full in the fullness of God.
EPHESIANS 3:17–19 MSG

UNDERSTAND:

- Do you feel that a life of "extravagant dimensions" is available to you? Why or why not?
- When you feel bored with your life, ask yourself, "Are my feet planted firmly on love? And if they're not, where *are* they planted?"

APPLY:

We have an extravagant God. In the words *The Message* uses for this passage of scripture, God "parcels out all heaven and earth" (verse 15) with a generous hand. Think about the vast range of

God's creation—from amoebas to whales, from African savannahs to the frozen arctic regions, from lakes, rivers, and seas that teem with life to the intricacy of human life. We live in a world of rich variety and infinite beauty, where all creation reflects the Creator's loving hand.

And yet in the midst of this wealth, we still manage to be bored. Our eyes grow blind to the wonder of the world. We lose the childlike attitude that looks at the world with curiosity and delight. Paul, the author of this letter to the church at Ephesus, tells us that the antidote to our numbed grown-up lives is one we may not have expected. We need to find a new perspective, one that is firmly planted in love.

PRAY:
Heavenly Friend, I ask that You restore to me a child's eyes and ears, so that even in the midst of a life that seems boring, I may perceive the wonder, mystery, and beauty of Your creation. Help me to take root in Your love so that I may grow into the person You want me to be.

I FEEL TRAPPED BY MY SITUATION

READ PSALM 124

KEY VERSE:
We escaped like a bird from a hunter's trap.
The trap is broken, and we are free!
PSALM 124:7 NLT

UNDERSTAND:
- Feeling trapped is not caused by the modern world's demands; thousands of years ago, the psalmist experienced this same claustrophobic, desperate feeling—which means the answers he found can also apply to us today.
- What circumstances in your life today feel like a trap?

APPLY:
Traps come in all shapes and sizes. Our jobs may have become traps, places that eat up our time and energy while giving nothing back to our hearts and minds. An unhealthy relationship may be another sort of trap, one where, in the words of the New Living Translation, we feel

as though people want to "[swallow] us alive" (verse 3). A self-destructive habit is still another sort of trap, and illness, depression, and lack of self-confidence are a few others.

Whatever trap has snared you, God can help you to escape. He will not let you be consumed or drowned by your circumstances. He is on your side—and since He is the One who made heaven and earth, He has all the power needed to set you free.

PRAY:
God, I don't see a way out of this situation—but I know You can do the impossible. You made the entire world, so I know You are strong enough to create new circumstances in my life.

I'M SO MAD!

READ PSALM 4:1–5

KEY VERSE:
Don't sin by letting anger control you.
Think about it overnight and remain silent.
PSALM 4:4 NLT

UNDERSTAND:

- Have you ever considered the relationship between anger and trust? Can you notice the effect anger has on your trust level—and vice versa, the effect trust has on your anger level?
- Notice that the Bible doesn't say that anger in itself is a sin. Instead, it says we go off track when we let anger control us.

APPLY:

The Hebrew and Greek words that our English Bibles translate as *sin* meant, literally, "the failure to hit the mark," like an arrow that shoots wide of its target. In more than one place, the Bible makes it clear that anger is not a sin— but anything that controls us, other than the

Spirit of God, can throw us off course, causing us to lose our focus on God and His love. We may have good reason to be angry, but anger has the power to be particularly destructive to those around us, leading to emotional and physical violence.

The psalmist gives us a practical recommendation in this passage of scripture: think about the situation overnight before you say anything. Rather than reacting in the heat of the moment, we need to think carefully about the appropriate words and actions to take.

PRAY:
Beloved Lord, You know how angry I feel about this situation. Help me to curb my anger so that it won't control me. Fill me with Your Spirit.

I NEED MORE PATIENCE

READ ROMANS 5:3–5

KEY VERSE:
We know how troubles can develop passionate patience in us, and how that patience in turn forges the tempered steel of virtue, keeping us alert for whatever God will do next.
ROMANS 5:3–4 MSG

UNDERSTAND:
- What in your life today requires patience on your part in order to deal with it?
- What do you think passionate patience looks like? Have you ever experienced it?

APPLY:

The words *patience* and *passionate* actually come from the same ancient word roots. The original meanings had to do with a willingness and commitment to endure pain or hardship. This is why the crucifixion is sometimes referred to as Christ's "Passion," because it required His willingness to bear pain, knowing that it would bring healing to all creation.

In verse 5 of this passage, *The Message* refers to "alert expectancy," meaning that we are to keep our eyes open so that we won't miss out on what God is doing. In the midst of life's challenges, we too can experience "passionate patience" if we keep in mind that God is using these circumstances to work out His will in our lives. It's easier to be patient when you know that God's loving and generous hand is doing something wonderful!

PRAY:
Jesus, thank You for Your passionate patience that made You willing to endure the cross on my behalf. I ask that You share Your patience with me. Keep me alert and expectant, waiting for God's miracles in my life.

I FEEL GUILTY FOR
LOSING MY TEMPER

READ GALATIANS 5:13–24

KEY VERSE:
*The fruit of the Spirit is love, joy,
peace, forbearance, kindness, goodness,
faithfulness, gentleness and self-control.*
GALATIANS 5:22–23 NIV

UNDERSTAND:

- When the Bible refers to the "flesh," it doesn't mean our physical bodies but rather the selfish, sinful side of human nature.
- Think about the last time you lost your temper. What was at the forefront of your mind at the time—your selfish desires or the Spirit of God?

APPLY:

That selfish side of human nature always wants its own way, so it gets angry when it doesn't get it. That in turn can lead to all sorts of other problems—hatred, arguments, jealousy, divisiveness, violence. As Jesus' followers, we can choose to put to death our selfish natures so that we can live a new life in the Spirit.

No one says it's easy to die to your selfishness, though. It's not. But this is where our focus should be. In other words, don't try to control your temper with sheer willpower. Instead, pull it up by its roots, killing the sin and selfishness that causes your temper. When you let the Spirit fill you, you won't have to work at being a nicer person, because your life will just naturally produce a new sort of fruit—love, joy, peace, patience, kindness, and self-control.

PRAY:
Jesus, I want to hang all my sin and selfishness on Your cross. Give me the courage, the discipline, and the commitment to die daily for You, so that Your Spirit can produce sweet fruits in my life.

I'M ANXIOUS ABOUT THE BILLS

READ PHILIPPIANS 4:6–7

KEY VERSE:
*Don't fret or worry. Instead of worrying, pray.
Let petitions and praises shape your worries
into prayers, letting God know your concerns.*
PHILIPPIANS 4:6 MSG

UNDERSTAND:
- Worrying and praying are opposite actions.
- Each time your worries about money come to mind, can you make a conscious effort to pray instead of worry?

APPLY:
When we worry, we imagine a bleak future that doesn't yet exist—that may, in fact, *never* exist. We picture all the terrible things that could happen if we aren't able to pay the bills. We feel inadequate to change things. We dwell on everything that may go wrong. Worry settles like a stone into the pit of our stomach, dulling our appreciation for life and robbing us of sleep at night.

In this passage of scripture, Paul is telling us that there's another option—instead of worrying, we can let petitions and praise shape our worries into prayers. As we make a conscious effort to do this, we will find that the peace of Christ pushes the worry out of our hearts. As a result, we may be able to perceive new solutions to our financial problems. God is concerned with each and every aspect of our lives, and He wants to help us with our money problems.

PRAY:
God, You know how worried I am about money. Help me to use this worry as a tool to turn my heart to You. Each time that worry jabs me again, may it be like a bell that calls my heart to prayer.

I'M WORRIED ABOUT MY CHILDREN

READ GENESIS 22:15–18

KEY VERSE:
"I'll make sure that your children flourish."
GENESIS 22:17 MSG

UNDERSTAND:
- What worries do you have today about your children?
- What happens to those worries if you imagine yourself placing your children into God's loving hands?

APPLY:
As parents, it's hard to understand how Abraham could have agreed to sacrifice his son, even if he was certain it was God's will. The point of this Old Testament story, though, is that God asks us to surrender *everything* to Him. He doesn't want us to hold back anything, even those most precious little people we love so much.

Surrendering our children to God's care may be something we have to do daily. Each stage of parenthood will require a new sort of surrender—from the moment when we first allow our child to walk without our steadying hands. . .to the day we wave goodbye as the school bus pulls away for the first day of kindergarten. . .to the first time our teenager takes the car out for an independent drive. But every step of the way, we can be confident that God will bless our children!

PRAY:
Lord, I give my children to You. I know You love them even more than I do—and I know Your care is all-encompassing, while mine is limited. Go with them and bless each moment of their lives. Even when I am no longer in this world to demonstrate my love to them, stay with them, I pray.

I CAN'T SLEEP

READ PROVERBS 3:21–26

KEY VERSE:
When you lie down, you will not be afraid;
when you lie down, your sleep will be sweet.
PROVERBS 3:24 NASB

UNDERSTAND:

- What keeps you awake at night? Is it fear and anxiety—or something else?
- How does wisdom apply to insomnia, as this passage of scripture suggests? Could it be the sleeping aid you need?

APPLY:
The Bible speaks of "wisdom" as though she were a person, making clear that wisdom is something far more than mere knowledge or intelligence. Some Bible scholars have even suggested that wisdom may be one of the roles Jesus took in the Old Testament. In any case, wisdom implies the deep sense of knowing that comes only from an intimate connection with God.

In this scripture passage, the author of the

book of Proverbs advises us to actively pursue wisdom, to keep it constantly with us like a piece of jewelry we wear around our necks. This constant soul connection with God will make us come alive spiritually—and it is the best antidote for sleepless nights. It will allow us to relax, confident that God has everything under control.

PRAY:
Lord of infinite wisdom, I want to follow only You. When sleep escapes me, may I still rest in Your presence. Fill my nighttime hours with the assurance of Your love.

I DON'T KNOW HOW TO HANDLE THIS CONFLICT

READ 2 TIMOTHY 2:23–25

KEY VERSE:
*Refuse foolish and ignorant speculations,
knowing that they produce quarrels.*
2 TIMOTHY 2:23 NASB

UNDERSTAND:

- Making biased and unfounded assumptions about others leads to conflicts.
- What assumptions have you made about your current situation? How might these assumptions be contributing to the conflict?

APPLY:

God does not ask us to simply give in to injustice. When Jesus found merchants abusing the temple by selling their wares there, He got angry, and He took action. But that kind of righteous anger has truth as its foundation. It is not the same as being quarrelsome.

Quarrels are generally petty, springing from small irritations that become magnified.

They're also caused by our failure to understand another's perspective. (There's a reason why a quarrel is also referred to as a "misunderstanding"!) Instead of waiting to get to the bottom of the situation, discovering the real truth, we leap to conclusions. Then we pass these faulty assumptions on to others, fanning the fires of conflict until the trivial problem grows into a major issue.

God calls us to refuse this kind of thinking and behavior, replacing it with kindness, patience, gentleness, and the willingness to discuss the situation with all the parties who are involved.

PRAY:
Heavenly Lord, this conflict has gotten out of hand. I ask Your forgiveness for all the ways that I have contributed to its growth—and I ask You now to show me opportunities for kindness, patience, and gentleness. May a willingness to listen to each other spread out from me to everyone who is involved.

I CAN'T STOP CRYING

READ REVELATION 21:3–5

KEY VERSE:
"He will wipe every tear from their eyes."
REVELATION 21:4 NLT

UNDERSTAND:
- What situation is bringing the tears to your eyes today?
- Can you believe that God is able to comfort you—even if you have to wait until you experience eternity?

APPLY:
In this world, death and loss are unavoidable. Every phase of life comes to an end, and each of the people we love will one day die. Tears are a very real part of human life.

This passage in the book of Revelation is describing a different reality, one that we've never experienced in this life. In this new reality, God dwells visibly with us, joined with us in an intimate relationship of belonging. We will no longer have any need for tears, because pain and death will have no place there.

It sounds too good to be true, doesn't it? God understands that feeling. Maybe that's why He told John, "Write this down, for what I tell you is trustworthy and true" (verse 5 NLT). Every tear we shed in this world will be comforted in heaven.

Pray:
I'm tired of crying, God. I feel as though all my tears should be gone by now, and yet they continue to fall. Thank You that You are here, even now in my sorrow. I give You my tears (right now, I have nothing else to give You), knowing that one day You will wipe them all dry.

I CAN'T SEEM TO FOCUS

READ PHILIPPIANS 3:12–16

KEY VERSE:
*God will clear your blurred
vision—you'll see it yet!*
PHILIPPIANS 3:15 MSG

UNDERSTAND:
- Goals are good focal points. They can keep us on track, even when we're exhausted or confused.
- What goals are shaping your life? Do they line up with God's will for you—or could some of them be contributing to your lack of focus?

APPLY:
A goal is a destination point we've chosen for our lives. The best goals are carefully considered in quiet moments. They're clearly defined, spelled out in concrete terms, so that even in the busiest, most confusing periods of our lives, we can still keep heading in the right direction. Without any goals, we'd just be wandering aimlessly through life.

As Christians, we are following Jesus. He is our goal, the end point we are striving to reach. Remember, though, what happened to Peter when he was walking toward Jesus on the Sea of Galilee—he took his eyes off his goal, and immediately he began to sink. The same thing happens to us, spiritually, when we lose our focus on Jesus. Things start to get blurry. Life seems confusing. We're not sure what we should be doing. We start to sink.

We all have moments like that, but this passage of scripture offers us hope and encouragement. God will sharpen our focus and clear our blurry eyes—so that once again, we can see Jesus.

PRAY:
Jesus, I'm coming to You. Show me the way. When life is confusing, help me to focus only on Your face.

I'M TIRED OF BEING SICK

READ PROVERBS 3:8–12

KEY VERSE:
*Your body will glow with health,
your very bones will vibrate with life!*
PROVERBS 3:8 MSG

UNDERSTAND:
- The Bible connects physical health with spiritual commitment. Have you experienced this in your life?
- This passage promises physical blessings, including good health—but it also implies that God's followers have learning opportunities whenever they face trials and other challenges. Has God taught you anything through your illness?
- Have you honored God by giving everything to Him, including your sickness?

APPLY:
When we're sick, we don't feel very shiny. Instead, we feel dull, lifeless. Our limbs feel heavy and weak. Our emotions are

weighed down by our bodies' condition, and discouragement and depression often set in.

But again and again throughout the Bible, God promises to bless those who give everything to Him. Whether it's our money, our children, or our health, however, surrender is the necessary first step. God can't bless our lives until they're truly His.

God may not heal our physical illness as quickly as we wish He would. In some cases, we may never experience physical healing. But God *always* wants to bless us. He wants us to glow with spiritual health. He wants the deepest structure of our souls to vibrate in tune with the Spirit's life.

PRAY:
Dearest Lord, I am so weary of being sick. I don't know how I can be of any use to You when I've been ill so long. I want so much to be well. But for today, I'll take the first step and give You my illness. I put my body in Your hands, trusting You to bless me in whatever ways I need most.

MY WORRIED IMAGINATION WON'T STOP

READ 2 CORINTHIANS 10:3–5

KEY VERSE:
Casting down imaginations, and every high thing that exalteth itself against the knowledge of God, and bringing into captivity every thought to the obedience of Christ.
2 CORINTHIANS 10:5 KJV

UNDERSTAND:
- What are the "weapons" referred to in this passage? Could scripture be one of our weapons against worry?
- What "strongholds" exist in you—fortified areas that have refused to surrender to Christ? How many of these strongholds are related to worry and anxiety?
- What does being obedient to Christ mean to you? What does it entail, in specific ways, in your daily life?

APPLY:
Worry and trust in God are incompatible—and

yet we often allow worry to take our minds captive. Controlling our thoughts is not easy. That's why this passage of scripture uses language that refers to warfare. The struggle is very real!

And yet modern psychologists agree with the apostle Paul that we have the ability to control our thoughts. They say to pay attention to "self-talk," that constant interior conversation that runs through our minds. When we catch ourselves saying negative things—*I know I'm going to fail at this. . .I don't think we have enough money. . .something bad is going to happen*—we can make a conscious effort to replace each thought with a positive affirmation, such as *With God's help, I'll do my best. . .God will supply all my needs. . .the future is in God's hands.*

PRAY:
Show me, Lord, the "forts" I've built against You in my thoughts. I ask that You help me to capture them and make them Yours.

I'M ASHAMED OF WHAT I DID

READ ROMANS 8:1–4

KEY VERSE:
*There is no condemnation for
those who belong to Christ Jesus.*
ROMANS 8:1 NLT

UNDERSTAND:

- What part of you was in control when you went astray? Can you identify the goal that had replaced Jesus in your mind?
- What does it mean to you to be freed from rules, while at the same time you belong to Jesus? Do you think Christians ever confuse "following the rules" with "following Jesus"? Do you?

APPLY:

Shame is different from guilt. Guilt acknowledges that we *did* something bad, while shame believes that we *are* bad. Jesus died so that we no longer need to feel shame.

We have all done things we later regret. Some of our mistakes are made innocently, with the best of intentions, but others happen because we are allowing our selfish natures to control our actions. And as Christians we are not immune to this problem. We still make mistakes. We may even do terrible things. When we do, we will have to suffer the consequences of our actions. We will experience guilt, and we will need to take decisive action to do whatever we can to make amends. But God does not condemn us. We need feel no shame.

Because we belong to God, the life-giving Spirit is at work in us, making us more and more like Jesus.

PRAY:
Jesus, I give You my shame. Take it from me and nail it to Your cross. May I be raised to new life in You.

I FEEL OUT OF CONTROL

READ MATTHEW 26:51–54

KEY VERSE:
*Then said Jesus unto him, Put up again thy
sword into his place: for all they that take
the sword shall perish with the sword.*
MATTHEW 26:52 KJV

UNDERSTAND:
- What happens when your emotions control your actions?
- If you think of your emotions as a "sword" you carry, have you ever wielded your weapon against others? Has that action ever turned back on you, wounding your own heart?

APPLY:
We know from other Gospel accounts of the incident described in this passage that Peter was the one who drew his sword and cut off the servant's ear. Peter frequently acted impulsively, as we see throughout the Gospels. He usually had good intentions—he clearly loved his Master—but he let his emotions

control him. As a result, he would speak and act before thinking.

Jesus was speaking about physical violence here, but we can also think of Peter's sword as a metaphor for his emotions. There's nothing wrong with having emotions, including negative emotions—but they should not control us. If we take them out of their proper place, they may hurt others. Ultimately, they may even destroy us.

Pray:
Jesus, forgive me for the times I have used my emotions as a weapon against those around me. Please heal those I have hurt. Help me to control my emotions better.

I'M SO DISAPPOINTED!

READ NUMBERS 23:19–23

KEY VERSE:
*"God is not human, that he should lie,
not a human being, that he should change
his mind. Does he speak and then not act?
Does he promise and not fulfill?"*
NUMBERS 23:19 NIV

UNDERSTAND:

- Which disappointments in your life are hardest to bear?
- When you are disappointed, where is your attention? Are you expecting God to do something for you that He failed to do? Or have you been placing your confidence in people who let you down?

APPLY:

Disappointment is inevitable in all our lives. People let us down; they promise they'll do something—and then they don't. Things we hope will happen don't happen.

But God promises that He will never

disappoint us. When He makes a promise, He always keeps it. He doesn't mislead us. So when He says He'll bless us, He will!

When disappointments start to pile up in our lives, it may be a call to notice where we're placing our confidence. Are we relying on God and His promises? Or are we expecting other people to make us happy in one way or another? Human beings, even the best of them, are fallible. Sooner or later, even the people who love us most will disappoint us. But God never will.

PRAY:
Remind me today, Holy Spirit, to rely only on God's promises. And when You do act, I will give You the credit, saying, "See what God has done!"

I'M NOT SURE I BELIEVE
IN GOD ANYMORE

READ LUKE 24:36–43

KEY VERSE:
*"Don't be upset, and don't let all these
doubting questions take over. Look at
my hands; look at my feet—it's really me.
Touch me. Look me over from head to toe."*
LUKE 24:38–39 MSG

UNDERSTAND:
- What makes you doubt God's reality?
  Are your doubts intellectual (based on
  things you *think*), or are they emotional
  (based on your inability to *feel* God)?
- Does your doubt make you feel guilty?
  Do you think God is angry with you if
  you doubt?
- How might you "touch" God in order
  to reassure your doubts?

APPLY:
We all have doubts sometimes about God's
reality. Doubt is normal. It's no sin to doubt.
But doubt that continues for a long time can

cause us pain. It can rob us of the peace and joy God wants us to experience. It can hamper our ability to be the people we want to be (the people God wants us to be).

You might think that the disciples, who had seen Jesus work miracle after miracle, would no longer doubt Him. That wasn't the case, though. Like all human beings, they could be filled with faith and love at one point in their lives—and then be terrified and doubting at another. And yet Jesus did not scold them for their doubt. Instead, He showed them Himself.

He longs to do the same with us. When doubts overcome us, He holds out His hands and says, "See? It's *Me*!"

PRAY:
Jesus, show me Yourself. Use even my doubts to draw me closer to You.

I FEEL BETRAYED

READ PSALM 41:9–13

KEY VERSE:
Even my close friend, someone I trusted, one who shared my bread, has turned against me.
PSALM 41:9 NIV

UNDERSTAND:
- Verse 12 (NIV) of this passage says, "Because of my integrity you uphold me." How might you demonstrate integrity in your own situation?
- When hurt and bitterness overcome you, can you make a conscious effort to turn to God?

APPLY:
There are few things that hurt more in life than being betrayed by someone we love, whether it's a friend, family member, or spouse. Of course all of us let each other down now and then; we're human and fallible. But betrayal goes deeper. It's a denial of the relationship we thought was so secure. It's like taking a step on what we took for granted was solid ground,

only to find ourselves falling into a chasm. It may make us doubt ourselves and our own worth. The emotional anguish may make us sink into depression.

When the psalmist experienced this, he took his pain to God. Instead of begging his betrayer to change back into the person he thought he could count on, he asked God to be the One to restore his sense of balance and security. He affirmed God's love for himself and praised God.

PRAY:
Lord, help me to have integrity even in the midst of this pain. Thank You that Your love will never fail me. You will never betray me. I praise You!

I TOLD A LIE—
AND NOW I'M SORRY!

READ PSALM 51:1–12

KEY VERSE:
*Wash me throughly from mine iniquity, and
cleanse me from my sin. For I acknowledge my
transgressions: and my sin is ever before me.*
PSALM 51:2–3 KJV

UNDERSTAND:
- Why do you think the psalmist said
  that his sin was against God, rather than
  the persons involved in the situation?
  Do you feel that your lie hurt God
  more than it did anyone else? Why or
  why not?
- What motive lay behind your lie?
- In verse 6 (KJV), the psalmist said that
  God desires "truth in the inward parts."
  What do you think he meant by that?

APPLY:
Lies can slip out so easily. We stray from the
truth for all sorts of reasons—to make ourselves
look better to others or to hide another even

worse sin. Sometimes we lie simply to make our conversation more interesting (we think) or to soothe another person's ego.

But the psalmist knew that truth is important to God, and he stressed that it's *inner* truth that's most vital for our relationship with God. Perhaps that's because we may begin to believe our own lies, creating a false self that doesn't match who we really are on the inside. How can we be close to God—or anyone else—when we're hiding ourselves?

The first step back to that inner truth is to acknowledge our lies and ask God's forgiveness. He is the only One who can wash away the falsehoods we've hidden behind.

PRAY:
Create in me a clean heart, God, and renew a right spirit within me. Don't cast me away from Your presence, and don't take Your Holy Spirit from me. Restore to me the joy of Your salvation, and hold me up with Your Spirit. (See verses 10–12 KJV.)

I'M JEALOUS

READ 1 CORINTHIANS 3:1–9

KEY VERSE:
*You are still worldly. For since there is jealousy
and quarreling among you, are you not worldly?
Are you not acting like mere humans?*
1 CORINTHIANS 3:3 NIV

UNDERSTAND:

- When Paul said he gave the people of Corinth milk rather than solid food, what do you think he meant?
- What makes you jealous? How might your jealousy be changed if you could see yourself as a coworker in God's service?
- Paul referred to various factions in the Corinthian church. Do you think jealousy plays any role in today's divided political arena?

APPLY:
Jealousy is a painful thing to feel. Usually it springs from our own feelings of inadequacy or insecurity. We are jealous of others' appearance,

talents, power, or popularity, feeling that whatever others possess will overshadow and diminish what we have. Or we may be jealous of the attention a friend or spouse shows to another individual. In both cases, we feel we will lose something that's vitally important to us, whether that's our own self-regard or the love of another person.

These are natural, human feelings. But Paul tells us in this passage of scripture that we are called to rise above the human perspective and instead see things from the Spirit's perspective. When we do so, we'll be able to see that in God we have everything we need. We are safe, secure, and valued. In His eyes, we are all equals, all called to work for the same goals, despite our individual ideas and perspectives. Together, in the words of the New International Version, we are "God's field, God's building" (verse 9).

Pray:
God of Love, help me to focus on You so that there's no room in my life for jealousy. Wean me from the spiritual milk I've needed, so that I can begin to eat Your solid food.

MY MIND IS FULL OF DOUBTS

READ MARK 9:17–29

KEY VERSE:
"I believe. Help me with my doubts!"
MARK 9:24 MSG

UNDERSTAND:

- In this passage from the Gospel of Mark, Jesus seems exasperated by the father's willingness to put up with his son's illness—but does He seem angry about the man's lack of faith?
- Do you think the man's doubts ever completely disappeared?

APPLY:

In this passage of scripture, Jesus shows human emotion in response to a situation. "How many times do I have to go over these things?" He says in *The Message.* "How much longer do I have to put up with this?" (verse 19). Most parents have said something similar to their children at one time or another!

And yet, reading this story nearly two thousand years after the event took place, we still don't understand what Jesus meant. We know that children continue to suffer illness, and God does not always heal them, even when their parents have a strong faith. Given the reality of our world, it's no wonder we still have doubts. The Bible is filled with promises of blessing and healing—but how can we believe those promises when we see so much suffering in our lives and in our world?

Perhaps the real message contained in this story is the example the father gives to us. He admits his doubt—and surrenders it to Jesus.

PRAY:
Jesus, like the father in this story, I am troubled and full of doubts. I need Your healing hand to touch a situation in my life. I believe in You—and I give You all my doubts.

I'M WORRIED
ABOUT MY PARENTS

READ ISAIAH 46:3–11

KEY VERSE:
*"And I'll keep on carrying you when
you're old. I'll be there, bearing
you when you're old and gray."*
ISAIAH 46:4 MSG

UNDERSTAND:
- What does it mean to be carried by God?
- When worries fill your mind about your parents, can you imagine them being held in God's arms?

APPLY:
It's hard to watch our parents age. These were the people who first loved us, who made our lives secure when we were children, and in some sense, they remain the foundation of our lives today. Our world shakes when we see them ill. We know that most of us will have to face our parents' deaths, sooner or later, but that doesn't make doing so any easier.

This passage from the book of Isaiah is

filled with promises we can apply to the lives of our parents. These promises remind us to look back at the past. No matter what hardships our parents faced, they survived them (or they wouldn't still be here today). God was with them. God carried them on His back since the day they were born—and He's not about to drop them now (verses 3–4).

The promises in these verses apply to us as well. When the day comes to say goodbye to our parents, we will be right where we were all along—safe on God's back. He will not drop us.

Pray:
Loving Father, I give my parents to You. I know that You have held them in Your arms all along, but I've been trying to pull them into my own arms instead. Help me to show them Your love. I thank You for their lives.

DEATH SCARES ME

Read John 11:20–43

Key Verse:
"I am the resurrection and the life. The one who believes in me will live, even though they die; and whoever lives by believing in me will never die. Do you believe this?"
John 11:25 NIV

Understand:

- Martha and Mary felt comfortable reproaching Jesus for what looked like a failure on His part. Have you ever felt as they did? Have you ever thought, *If only God had stepped in and stopped this from happening! Where was He?* Did you feel free to express those feelings? Why or why not?

- Why do you think Jesus wept, when He must have known He was about to bring Lazarus back to life?

Apply:

People in earlier times lived with death much more closely than we do today. Modern medicine extends our lives and heals diseases that once killed so many people. Today, death seems unnatural to us, like something we should all be able to avoid, and yet that is clearly not the case. Death is an inescapable reality. It's the great mystery that we all face—and it's only natural to fear the unknown.

In this story from the Gospel of John, Jesus doesn't deny that death is real. Its reality makes Him cry, despite the fact that in a few moments He will bring His friend back to life. We too will mourn and cry when death touches our lives—the pain is inescapable—but at the same time, we can hear Jesus' words: "I am the resurrection and the life. The one who believes in me will live, even though they die."

Pray:
Thank You, Jesus, that You used Lazarus's death to teach all of us that You are the Lord of both life and death. I'm still afraid—but I know that whatever happens, You are with me.

I FEEL INADEQUATE

READ 2 CORINTHIANS 12:7–10

KEY VERSE:
My grace is sufficient for thee:
for my strength is made perfect in weakness.
2 CORINTHIANS 12:9 KJV

UNDERSTAND:

- Scripture doesn't tell us what Paul's "thorn in the flesh" (verse 7 KJV) was, but we don't really need to know. What is *your* thorn in your flesh? What is it that makes you feel inadequate?
- Look back on your life. Can you see occasions when you experienced God's strength in the midst of your own weakness?

APPLY:

No matter how talented, skilled, or intelligent we are, all of us have flaws and weaknesses that hold us back from living our lives the way we wish we could. These weaknesses may get in the way of our personal lives, our professional lives, or our spiritual lives. We wish God would simply take them away from us, and we may even beg Him to do so. But often our prayers seem to go unanswered.

Following Jesus, however, does not mean we will magically become perfect people. All of us will continue to suffer in some way, whether from an illness, a character flaw, or a lack of ability in some vital area of our lives. We ask ourselves, *If God loves me, why won't He step in and take this problem away from me? Hasn't He promised over and over that He will bless me?* But sometimes, strange as it seems, the problem *is* the blessing. It forces us to see how much we need God.

PRAY:
I wish I didn't have to bear this flaw of mine, Lord. But since I do, I'll give it to You. Use me, with all my flaws, however You want. Be strong in my weakness.

I NEED SOME TIME ALONE

READ MARK 1:32–39

KEY VERSE:
*In the early morning, while it was still dark,
Jesus got up, left the house, and went away to a
secluded place, and was praying there.*
MARK 1:35 NASB

UNDERSTAND:
- Many things that happened in Jesus' life were never recorded in the Gospels—so we have to assume that what *was* recorded was written for a reason. Why do you think the authors of the Gospels tell us again and again that Jesus sought out times to be alone?
- What relationship do you think existed between Jesus' alone times and His times of ministry?

APPLY:
The Gospels make it clear that Jesus had an extremely busy life. He and His disciples seemed to travel constantly from one place to another, and always, crowds were following

them, pressing around Jesus, clamoring for His attention.

Having just finished a busy day of healing, knowing that another equally busy day lay ahead, Jesus would have needed a good night's sleep. He knew, however, that He also needed something else—time alone—and so He got up very early in the morning in order to have that time.

When our days are busy, we sometimes neglect our times of solitude. *I just don't have time now*, we tell ourselves. *Alone time will have to wait until things calm down a little.* Jesus, however, shows us by example that the busier our lives are, the more we need to include those quiet moments of solitude. Without them, we won't have the strength we need to do His work.

PRAY:
Jesus, help me to remember to make time to be alone with You. I can't face my busy life without You.

I FEEL FOOLISH

READ GALATIANS 1:10–24

KEY VERSE:

Am I now trying to win the approval of human beings, or of God? Or am I trying to please people? If I were still trying to please people, I would not be a servant of Christ.
GALATIANS 1:10 NIV

UNDERSTAND:

- Paul's actions in the past were far worse than mere foolishness. If you had done what he did, do you think you would have had the courage to become a prominent leader of the faith?
- Does your sense of foolishness hold you back from doing the work of God? If so, in what ways?

APPLY:

All of us feel foolish sometimes. We do things we fear will make us appear stupid. No matter how much we wish we could erase our actions, there they still are, looming in our own minds long after others may have forgotten them.

Often, we allow our sense of foolishness to hold us back. We hesitate to call any further attention to ourselves. (In fact, we may wish we could crawl into the woodwork and disappear completely!)

Paul's actions against the early Church weren't mere foolishness; they were violent and hateful. And yet because he was now a servant of Christ, he had to lay aside his worry about others' opinions of him.

That's so hard to do! But we too, like Paul, are called by God to serve Jesus. That means we have to set aside our sense of our own foolishness and instead focus on pleasing Him. His opinion is the only one that matters.

PRAY:
Today, Jesus, please remind me, again and again, that I am Your servant. Help me to forget what others may think of me. I want to please You— and I want to live in such a way that in the end, regardless of how foolish I am, others will praise You because of me.

I CAN'T TAKE THE STRESS

READ PSALM 55:6–8, 16–17, 22

KEY VERSE:
Cast your cares on the LORD
and he will sustain you.
PSALM 55:22 NIV

UNDERSTAND:

- Have you ever wished you could simply fly away, like a bird, from the demands of your life? What circumstances in your life cause those feelings?
- How might you find practical ways to cast your cares on the Lord? What actions might that involve?
- When the stress in your life seems overwhelming, would it help you to set your phone or computer to remind you to pause, just for a moment, and pray?

APPLY:

The psalmist expressed in these verses a feeling that most of us have had at one time or another: *If only I could run away from my life! If only I could just be alone, somewhere safe* and quiet where nothing was expected of me! Although we do need to find moments to be alone, even in the midst of our busy lives, it's usually not possible to totally escape the stress and pressure each day brings. Apparently the author of this psalm couldn't escape his life's demands either.

Instead, he shows us another way: throughout his stressful days—"evening, morning and noon" (verse 17 NIV)—he called to God for help. When the stress in our lives seems unmanageable, we need to follow his example. We don't need to wait to be alone to call out to God. It only takes a moment to cast our stress into God's hands, again and again and again throughout our busy days.

PRAY:
Strong Lord, take my stress and carry it for me. May I feel a new sense of lightness, even in the midst of my life's demands.

I'M EXHAUSTED

READ ISAIAH 40:28–31

KEY VERSE:
Those who trust in the LORD will find new strength. They will soar high on wings like eagles. They will run and not grow weary. They will walk and not faint.
ISAIAH 40:31 NLT

UNDERSTAND:
- Do you ever feel guilty for being tired? These verses make it clear that exhaustion is a normal part of human life.
- Have you ever considered that if we had the energy to do everything we want, we might forget to turn to God? Our weakness reminds us that we need Him.

APPLY:
Life can be exhausting. Whether we're parents coping with the demands of young children, busy professionals with schedules crammed with meetings, or retired folk with to-do lists

as long as our arms, we all sometimes feel as though we just don't have the energy to go on.

And yet we have to. Although we can take steps to simplify our lives, letting go of what's unnecessary, some tasks are unavoidable. Children and elderly parents need care. Our jobs have demands that are simply part of the work we've been hired to do. Meals need to be prepared, houses cleaned, lawns tended, and errands run. Life doesn't stop because we're tired!

Humans have experienced weariness since the beginning of time. And over the long centuries, God has promised us His strength. "Trust Me," He says. "Let Me do the heavy lifting. I am the Source of all your energy. Let Me give you what you need to face your life today."

PRAY:

God of strength and love, thank You for caring so much about me. You know how tired I feel. You understand—and You want to help. So today I'll lean on You. I want to soar on Your wings.

I FEEL SO HELPLESS

READ JOHN 15:1–8

KEY VERSE:
*"Live in me. Make your home in me just as
I do in you. In the same way that a branch
can't bear grapes by itself but only by
being joined to the vine, you can't bear
fruit unless you are joined with me."*
JOHN 15:4 MSG

UNDERSTAND:

- What would it look like if you were to make your home in Jesus?
- Examine your life. Do your helpless feelings come because you have been trying to bear fruit without being joined to Jesus?
- Jesus speaks in these verses of pruning the vine so that it can bear more fruit. Do you feel that He has "pruned" you? In what ways?
- Do you think of "pruning" as a negative, painful experience? Does it have to be? Is that what Jesus is indicating in these verses?

APPLY:

Again and again, God tells us in the Bible, "Stop trying to do things on your own! I want to do amazing things in your life—but I need you to get out of My way!"

Of course we feel helpless sometimes—because we *are*! No matter how much we try, we are powerless to change certain circumstances. We can keep pulling and tugging, straining with effort day after day, and we'll still accomplish absolutely nothing. It's so frustrating!

But Jesus tells us that's an unnatural way to live. It's like a branch thinking it can continue to bear fruit after it's been cut off from the vine; it just won't happen. The natural way, the way of being we were created to experience, is to simply relax into Him and allow His life to flow through us, out into the world.

PRAY:

Jesus, You know how helpless this situation makes me feel. Help me to stop trying to be in control of the situation, so that You can take over. I want to make my home in You so that You can make Your home in me.

MY HOPE IS GONE

READ ZECHARIAH 9:9–12

KEY VERSE:
*Return to your fortress, you prisoners
of hope; even now I announce that I
will restore twice as much to you.*
ZECHARIAH 9:12 NIV

UNDERSTAND:
- When you feel hopeless, in what way are you a "prisoner of hope"? What might freedom mean for you?
- What do you think the fortress is that's referred to in the key verse? Can you think of "fortresses" in your own life where you might be able to return for safety?

APPLY:
Sometimes life looks pretty hopeless. Whether we're facing a personal problem or considering the state of our world, the situation gives us little cause for hope. As hard as we try, we just can't see any solutions.

When that happens, we often become

afraid to hope any longer. Because we've had our hopes dashed so often, hope becomes something painful. It seems like a prison, a trap that holds us back from facing reality, rather than something positive that gives us courage.

But the kind of hope the Bible talks about isn't merely wishing that things will turn out the way we want them to. Instead, it's a confident expectation that no matter how bad things look, God is behind the scenes working out something better than anything we could ever come up with on our own. The result may not be what we wished would happen— but ultimately, God tells us, it will be twice as good!

PRAY:
God of hope, show me Your fortress where I will be safe during this time when it's so hard to hold on to hope. I'll stop looking for my own solutions— and instead wait for You to act. My hope is only in You.

MY KIDS ARE DRIVING ME CRAZY

READ EPHESIANS 4:1–6

KEY VERSE:
Walk in a manner worthy of the calling with which you have been called, with all humility and gentleness, with patience, showing tolerance for one another in love.
EPHESIANS 4:1–2 NASB

UNDERSTAND:
- Have you ever considered that it takes humility to be a parent? How might a lack of humility be contributing to your frustration with your children?
- Do you ever think of your children as fellow members of Christ's body, sharing with you in the Spirit's life? How might your attitudes change if you were to keep this idea at the forefront of your consciousness?
- Why do you think Paul reminded his readers that he was in prison as he wrote these words? Does your life as a parent ever feel like a prison you wish you could escape?

APPLY:

Being a parent is hard work. In fact, it's one of the most (if not *the* most) challenging, frustrating, crazy-making jobs we'll ever face. Children's demands on our time and attention are relentless. As parents, we'd like to feel we're in control. We may think that's what it means to be a good parent, exercising discipline over our children, and so we're frustrated and upset when our children seem uncontrollable. Of course, it *is* our job to teach our children, using loving discipline to shape them into responsible adults—but we can't reason with them the way we would with another adult. We can't tell our newborn to stop waking us up in the middle of the night. . .or our toddler to stop asking a million questions a day. . .or our teenager to stop being so emotional.

All we can do is follow Paul's advice: be humble, patient, tolerant, diligent—and do our best to be as good a parent to our children as God is to us.

PRAY:

Divine Parent, when my children drive me crazy, remind me that they share with me in Your love and life. Use me to demonstrate to them Your loving care.

MY MOTHER IS DRIVING ME CRAZY

READ EPHESIANS 4:23–32

KEY VERSE:
Be angry, and yet do not sin.
EPHESIANS 4:26 NASB

UNDERSTAND:

- The New Testament has many verses about how we are to interact with others within the body of Christ. Have you ever considered that these words apply to your relationship with family members as well?

- How might you handle your anger without sinning? What do you think Paul meant when he gave that advice?

APPLY:

Of course, it may not be your mother who annoys you. It could be your mother-in-law or your sister. It could be some other family member. But most of us have at least one close relation who just drives us crazy!

When Paul wrote this letter to the church

at Ephesus, he had a good understanding of human nature. He knew how people act when they are in close relationship with one another, and he knew that it's not all happy, fuzzy feelings—not by any means! Inevitably, we're going to get angry with the people we love.

But Paul reminds us that anger does not have to lead to sin. We don't have to allow it to hurt others. Instead, day by day, as we interact with family members, we need to be "renewed in the spirit of [our] mind," putting on the "new self" He has called us to be (verses 23–24 NASB).

PRAY:
Give me more patience with this person, Lord. Help me to be kinder, more tenderhearted, forgiving her for her foibles as You have forgiven me (verse 32).

MY SPOUSE IS DRIVING ME CRAZY

READ 1 CORINTHIANS 13:4–7

KEY VERSE:
Love is patient, love is kind.
1 CORINTHIANS 13:4 NASB

UNDERSTAND:

- It's easy to blame our spouse for our negative reactions. If you look at the last time you were upset with your spouse, though, can you see the role that your own selfishness played? How might you have been seeking your own way?

- What do you think verse 5 (NASB) means when it says that love does not "take into account a wrong suffered"? What "wrongs" committed by your spouse have you added up in an "account"?

APPLY:

The people we love the most also have the ability to upset us the most. They get on our nerves. Their little habits bug us. They hurt our feelings. Day after day, week after week, we tend to add up their offenses, keeping score, using them to justify our own hurtful actions. If our spouse did such and such, then surely we have the right to do *this* or *that*!

Luckily for us, that's not the way God treats us. He shows us what real love looks like—patient, kind, unselfish, enduring. He doesn't keep track of everything we've done wrong and hold each thing against us. Instead, He rejoices in all we do that's true and beautiful.

How might our marriages change if we were to make a conscious effort to love our spouses the way God loves us?

PRAY:
Today, Lord of love, bring to my attention all the things my spouse does that are good, truthful, and loving. Help me to be more patient with the actions that annoy or hurt me. Give me the strength to be kind.

MY LIFE IS JUST TOO HARD

READ JAMES 1:2–6

KEY VERSE:
*When your faith is tested, your
endurance has a chance to grow.*
JAMES 1:3 NLT

UNDERSTAND:

- How might you consider the troubles that come your way a chance for great joy (verse 2)? Does this seem like a contradiction that's too hard for you to surmount?
- If you had greater wisdom (verse 5), do you think you would be able to better see the joy interwoven with the trouble? Why or why not?

APPLY:
Sometimes the Bible seems to ask too much of us. Looking at trouble as an opportunity for joy (verse 2) is over the top!

And yet James, the author of these verses, asks us to consider another perspective. The challenges we face in life often threaten to take from us something we value, whether our pride, our money, or the companionship of people we love. It's natural to value these things, but when we place our faith in any of them, rather than in God, we are bound to feel unsettled by life's circumstances. The changing tides of life will blow us back and forth, tossing us and shaking us (verse 6).

When we are truly secure in God, though, we can head into the wind, our course unshaken. Despite any pain, we will still know God's joy, as steady as ever. Our strength and endurance will grow.

Pray:
God, my life seems too hard to bear right now. Show me Your joy, a steady thread woven through the challenges. Remind me that when my faith is in You, You will make me strong enough to endure whatever demands I face.

MY FEELINGS ARE HURT

READ EPHESIANS 6:10–18

KEY VERSE:
*Be strong in the Lord and in his mighty
power. Put on the full armor of God.*
EPHESIANS 6:10–11 NIV

UNDERSTAND:

- When your feelings are hurt, do you
ever consider that there may be something going on behind the scenes in the
spiritual realm? How might the devil
use your hurt feelings to further the
forces of evil in the world?
- Do you think of the person who hurt
you as an enemy? Can you see that
your struggle is not with that individual
but rather with a larger, spiritual reality?

APPLY:
The people we care about have the power to
hurt us—and whether they intend to or not,
sooner or later, inevitably, they injure our
feelings (as we do theirs!). We can allow the
hurt to drive us apart, turning loved ones into

enemies. But that's not what God wants, and if we allow it to happen, then we have allowed the devil to win. God's purpose for our lives is peace and harmony with others; He wants us to learn to walk more and more steadily in His love.

And so when our feelings are hurt, we need to protect our hearts with God's shining armor of love, rather than the devil's rusty shield of bitterness and anger. It's not easy. That's why this scripture reminds us to stay alert and pray for one another (verse 18). God's Word and Spirit will be the protection we need.

PRAY:
Lord, You know the hurt I'm feeling. But I ask You to make me strong in Your power. Put Your belt of truth around my waist, shield my heart with Your breastplate of righteousness, remind me to wear Your shoes of peace, and help me to cling tight to Your shield of faith.

THE FUTURE SCARES ME

READ PSALM 139:3–15

KEY VERSE:
*I look behind me and you're there,
then up ahead and you're there, too—your
reassuring presence, coming and going.*
PSALM 139:5 MSG

UNDERSTAND:

- When you look back on your life, can you see the way God has been with you, ever since your conception in your mother's womb? Does this help you to face the future with greater confidence?
- Do you truly believe that God has the future in His hands—or do you doubt His power to manage all of time, past, present, and future? How might your feelings change if you could truly trust in God's presence throughout all time?

APPLY:
A children's picture book, *The Runaway Bunny* by Margaret Wise Brown, tells a similar story as the first verses in this passage of scripture.

The little bunny thinks of one situation after another where he might escape his mother's love. He imagines himself becoming a bird or a fish or a boat—and each time, his mother assures him that whatever he becomes and wherever he goes, she will be right there with him, fitting into the scenario in whatever way is required for her to stay close to him.

God's love for us is the same as the mother bunny's for her child. No matter what happens to us in the future, no matter where we go or what we become, He will be there, present in the circumstances. He sees our future as clearly as He sees in the past—and He is already there, up ahead, waiting for us.

PRAY:
Thank You, Spirit of love, that the future can take me nowhere that will ever lead me out of Your presence.

I WISH SOMEONE UNDERSTOOD ME

READ PSALM 139:1–2

KEY VERSE:
*I'm an open book to you; even from
a distance, you know what I'm thinking.*
PSALM 139:2 MSG

UNDERSTAND:

- Why do you think others are unable to understand you? Is the fault theirs or yours—or no one's? Can you forgive them for their lack of understanding?
- Are you comfortable knowing that God knows your most private thoughts, even when He seems distant from you? Does His understanding comfort you— or scare you? Why?

APPLY:
All of us have moments when we feel as though no one in the entire world understands us. It's a lonely feeling! We all need the sense that at least one other person understands our thoughts and feelings. That understanding

would make us feel we're not strange or bad or unacceptable in some way. Without it, we feel as though there might be something wrong with us. We feel sad, rejected, alone.

In reality, if we had the courage to share our hearts with others, we'd probably find that they can understand more than we think they might. But until we have the confidence we need to reveal our true selves, we can allow God's understanding to heal our wounded hearts. Even if we think He is far away, even when we reject Him, He understands what we're going through. He is the Friend who will never fail us. He's on our side.

PRAY:
My God, I thank You that You understand me, even when no one else seems to. I open my heart to You. I don't want to hold back any part of myself from You. Teach me to rely more and more on Your friendship.

I CAN'T FORGIVE
WHAT THEY DID TO ME

READ MATTHEW 6:9–14

KEY VERSE:
*If ye forgive men their trespasses,
your heavenly Father will also forgive you.*
MATTHEW 6:14 KJV

UNDERSTAND:
- What offenses that you've experienced from others seem unforgiveable? Why?
- Does the reminder that you need God's forgiveness give you a better sense of perspective about the things others have done that hurt you? Why or why not?

APPLY:
When Jesus taught His followers how to pray, He included the line "Forgive us our debts, as we forgive our debtors" (verse 12 KJV), and then, after saying amen, He reinforced that message by repeating how important forgiveness is to the kingdom of heaven. When He links God's forgiveness of our sins to our ability to forgive

others, it may sound as though God will punish us for our hard hearts—but hard, scientific research has found that people who are unable to forgive hurt themselves, physically and emotionally. Jesus knew that the spiritual effects are just as detrimental.

Forgiving others doesn't mean that what the other person did to hurt us doesn't matter or that it was okay for them to do what they did. Forgiveness *does* mean being willing to let go of whatever happened and move on. It allows us to move into a place of greater freedom, a place where God has space to bless us.

PRAY:
Jesus, help me to live as You did when You were on earth. Help me to forgive those who have hurt me. I want to be part of Your kingdom.

I FEEL TOO WEAK TO COPE

READ NEHEMIAH 8:9–12

KEY VERSE:
*"Don't be dejected and sad, for the
joy of the LORD is your strength!"*
NEHEMIAH 8:10 NLT

UNDERSTAND:

- Have you ever felt that God is asking too much of you? That you're not strong enough to live up to His expectations?
- What part do your emotions play in your sense of weakness?
- How can you create a small celebration today, so that you can experience God's joy? Nehemiah suggested indulging in special foods and drinks—and also sharing gifts of food with others. Is there someone you could invite to share a meal with you? If so, notice what happens to your feelings of weakness.

APPLY:

How funny—when God's people heard His words for them, they started to cry! And yet don't we often respond in a similar way to God's voice? We feel we are too weak to cope with the demands He has placed on us. "We're only human," we whine. "He can't expect us to actually live all the time in the way the Bible describes!"

God doesn't want to make us cry! His very nature is one of love and joy, and He wants us to experience both. He's not concerned with whether we're weak or strong in our own abilities and resources; He just wants us to listen to His words. . .and then celebrate!

As this passage of scripture indicates, celebrations are not meant to be private affairs. They're occasions to share with others. Doing so just might lift our sense of weakness, replacing it with the joy of our Lord.

PRAY:
God of joy, take my sense of depression and helplessness and replace it with Your strength. Turn me outward, toward others. Help my life be a celebration of Your love.

I FEEL UNSAFE

Read Deuteronomy 31:3–6

Key Verse:
*"Be strong. Take courage. Don't be intimidated.
Don't give them a second thought because
God, your God, is striding ahead of you.
He's right there with you. He won't let
you down; he won't leave you."*
Deuteronomy 31:6 msg

Understand:

- What in your life makes you feel unsafe? Is it an emotional, spiritual, or physical threat?
- What steps can you take to be safe? Can you ask God to guide you to the steps that need to be taken?

Apply:
Feeling unsafe is a terrible experience. We all need a basic sense of security in order to thrive. It's important to determine where the danger lies (and whether it's real or imagined) and then to take the necessary steps to ensure that we are safe. Often, however, our emotions

are what stand in the way of our taking the bold, assertive action that's necessary. We get intimidated, and we freeze in our tracks, afraid to make the necessary moves.

When we're in physical danger, God will be with us, helping us to find ways to protect ourselves (whether that's calling the police, leaving an abusive relationship, or moving to a safer neighborhood). God also wants to protect us from emotional and spiritual danger, guiding us to decisive action that will take us out of danger. He is right there with us, and He will never let us down!

PRAY:
God of courage, guide me to the steps I need to take to protect myself. Thank You that You are already striding ahead of me, ready to show me the way.

I'M LONELY

READ PSALM 23

KEY VERSE:
*Even when I walk through the darkest valley,
I will not be afraid, for you are close beside me.*
PSALM 23:4 NLT

UNDERSTAND:
- What connection between loneliness and fear, if any, do you feel in your life?
- What does it mean to you that the Lord is your Shepherd? Can you grasp that concept?
- Do you believe that God is close beside you, no matter how dark life may seem? Why or why not?

APPLY:
Loneliness is not the same as solitude. Solitude is a sense of joyful engagement with ourselves and with the Holy Spirit that we experience while being alone. It's good for us. Loneliness, however, is destructive, not only emotionally and spiritually but physically as well; scientific research has found that lonely

people suffer more physical illnesses.

Life is full of dark valleys, stretches of time when for one reason or another, we feel very alone. It might be a work situation. . .a family crisis. . .the death of a loved one. . .a serious illness. . .or merely the sense that we have no one with whom to share both the good and bad of our lives. God does not want us to be lonely, though. Not only does He want us to find ways to connect with others, but He also wants us to know that He is always with us.

PRAY:
Thank You, Shepherd of my soul, that You are always with me, guiding me through even the darkest valley. Give me all that I need to nourish my soul—including the companionship of others— so that I can be all that You want me to be.

I'M FRUSTRATED

READ PROVERBS 3:5–8

KEY VERSE:
*Trust in the LORD with all your heart and
do not lean on your own understanding.*
PROVERBS 3:5 NASB

UNDERSTAND:
- Can you see a relationship between frustration and trust? If so, what do you think it is? How does one affect the other?
- If you let go of your sense that you are in control of your own life, what happens to your frustration?
- How might you acknowledge God in all your ways (verse 6)?

APPLY:
Frustrate comes from the same Latin word as *fraud*. Both words originally had to do with being cheated out of something that is deserved. And isn't that what we feel when we are frustrated—that something we *deserved* has failed to happen? Whether it's something

we want to do that we just can't seem to accomplish. . .or other people acting in ways we don't like. . .or circumstances not falling into place the way we'd hoped, frustration robs us of our sense of control. We feel as though our lives have gone off course. We believe we *needed* something to happen, but it didn't!

When we're frustrated, though, odds are pretty good that we're leaning on our own understanding rather than God's. Trust means that we put *everything* in God's hands—our abilities, other people's actions, even the weather—allowing Him to straighten things out in His time, in His way.

PRAY:
God of wisdom, when I feel frustrated, help me not to rely so much on my own understanding of my life. Remind me to trust You more so that You can make my way lead straight to You.

I HATE THE WAY I LOOK

READ SONG OF SOLOMON 4

KEY VERSE:
*"You are altogether beautiful, my darling,
and there is no blemish in you."*
SONG OF SOLOMON 4:7 NASB

UNDERSTAND:

- When you read this passage of scripture, how do you feel? Are you comfortable with the sensual language that some Bible scholars apply to the soul's relationship with God? Why or why not?
- Try to imagine that God is passionately in love with you. How does that make you feel?

APPLY:

We are so hard on ourselves. Our society tells us in a host of different ways—from television commercials to Facebook memes, from movies and television programs to magazine articles—that we need to look a certain way. If we don't, if we have lumps and bulges on our hips, crooked teeth, or a big nose, we feel that we don't measure up. Our body parts are either too big or too small; our hair is too straight or too curly; our skin color is too dark or too pale. When you think about it, it's downright silly! People are *meant* to look different from each other. It's what makes them so interesting.

And when God looks at us, He sees no blemishes. In His eyes, we are altogether lovely! So if God likes the way we look, why do we care so much about what the world thinks?

Pray:

Darling God, Lover of my soul, thank You that You love me just the way I am. Teach me not to regard myself from the world's perspective. Help me instead to see myself through Your eyes.

I WISH I COULD LOSE WEIGHT

READ 1 CORINTHIANS 10:23–31

KEY VERSE:
Whether you eat or drink or whatever
you do, do it all for the glory of God.
1 CORINTHIANS 10:31 NIV

UNDERSTAND:
- When you eat and drink, do you think about God's glory?
- What are your motives for losing weight?
- Why might God want you to lose weight? How would it affect your ability to serve Him?

APPLY:
One of the messages the world gives us is that we all need to be slender. Women in particular feel the pressure to strive endlessly to have the sort of Barbie-doll body we've come to think of as perfection. That type of body, however, is impossible for most women. And no matter how much weight is lost, it usually will be gained back once we resume normal eating patterns.

Meanwhile, God doesn't care how much we weigh. Fat or thin, He loves us just the same.

But although He allows us the right to do anything we want, including overeating or eating the wrong sorts of food, He does want us to realize that some behaviors, including consuming too many calories and not exercising enough, are not beneficial to our health. So instead of dieting, we might try simply being aware, each time we open our mouths to eat or drink, of whether we are pleasing God.

PRAY:
Help me, loving God, to stop caring so much about what the world thinks of me—and instead to care more about giving You glory. May my eating and drinking be constructive, joyful actions that make me more able to serve You.

I HATE FEELING SO AWKWARD!

READ PSALM 54:1–4

KEY VERSE:
Surely God is my help; the Lord
is the one who sustains me.
PSALM 54:4 NIV

UNDERSTAND:
- Why do you feel awkward? Is it physical clumsiness that embarrasses you—or are you uncomfortable in social settings?
- What connection do you feel between your sense of awkwardness and your need to impress others?
- Do you feel that others are judging you harshly, rather than accepting you just as you are? How does this contribute to your sense of awkwardness?

APPLY:
Back in the Middle Ages, we might have described ourselves as "awky" (rather than "awkward"), and we would have meant that something about us was turned in the wrong direction, preventing us from moving through

life smoothly. Today, when we feel awkward, we still have the sense that something about us isn't the way it should be. Some behavior, whether our body's movements or our interactions with others, trips us up. We feel as though we're trying to walk with our feet on backward!

We all have that feeling sometimes, but even so, people often judge others harshly for their awkward behaviors. When we're on the receiving end of this judgment, we cringe with embarrassment. We feel attacked, ashamed, destroyed.

But God is there to help us! No matter how awkward we may be, He will vindicate us. In Him, we will find our true worth.

PRAY:
Sustain me, Lord, with Your hand. When I trip, help me up. When I fumble, help me pick up the broken pieces. When I bumble through life like a bull in a china shop, ease my embarrassment with Your love. Teach me to rely on You.

I'VE FALLEN OUT OF LOVE

READ PHILIPPIANS 4:5–9

KEY VERSE:
*Whatever is true, whatever is noble, whatever
is right, whatever is pure, whatever is lovely,
whatever is admirable—if anything is excellent
or praiseworthy—think about such things.*
PHILIPPIANS 4:8 NIV

UNDERSTAND:
- Do you see any connection between verses 4–7 and the verses that follow? Why or why not?
- How does your spiritual life intersect with your love relationship? Does it? Can you ask God to dwell in this relationship?

APPLY:
All long-term relationships have their ups and downs, and most married folks would have to admit that at one time or another they fell out of love with their spouses. Hurt feelings may come between us, or we may simply fall out of step with each other. Little annoying habits we

once overlooked start to grate on our nerves. We miss the happiness and romance we once experienced together.

Most long-married couples will fall out of love and back again more than once in their lives together, and each time, their marriage grows stronger. In the meantime, when our love may seem dead, we can take the advice found in these verses: Rejoice in the Lord. Be gentle with our spouse. Stop worrying and start praying about the situation. Focus on the things we still like about our spouse. Rely on God's peace in our hearts.

PRAY:
God of all love, I thank You for my spouse. Help me to focus on all that is good and true and admirable in this person I married. Draw me closer to You through this time when my love feels dead. Renew my love, and fill me with Your peace.

I'M SO CONFUSED!

READ PROVERBS 3:1–7

KEY VERSE:
Trust GOD from the bottom of your heart;
don't try to figure out everything on your own.
PROVERBS 3:5 MSG

UNDERSTAND:
- Trust applies to so many different situations and emotions! How do you think greater trust might affect your sense of confusion?
- Often we forget to read Bible verses in their full context. What meaning, if any, do think the other verses in this passage add to the key verse?

APPLY:
No one likes to feel confused. For centuries, the literal meaning of the word has been "mixed up"—everything tangled up together, with no sense of clarity or order—but the implied meaning has also been (according to the Online Etymology Dictionary) "troubled, embarrassed, dejected, downcast, undone,

defeated." No wonder we don't like to be confused!

The wise person who wrote these proverbs knew the answer to all our painful confusion. When we let go of our need to figure out things with our own powers of reasoning, we can listen for God's quiet voice speaking from within the turmoil. When we run to Him, we will escape any evil our confusion might cause. If we truly trust God to be in control, we don't really need to figure everything out!

PRAY:
Lord, I want to be filled with love for You; keep me loyal to You and to Your Word. Help me to lay aside my confusion and instead trust You from the bottom of my heart.

I CAN'T COPE MUCH LONGER

Read Philippians 4:12–14

Key Verse:
*I can do all this through
him who gives me strength.*
Philippians 4:13 niv

Understand:
- What does "coping" mean to you? Do you have unrealistic expectations of yourself?
- How might you find contentment in your current situation? What would you need to have happen?
- Verse 14 speaks of others who were willing to share the apostle Paul's troubles. Is there anyone in your life willing to do that for you? If so, does that help you feel as though you can cope a little better?

Apply:
According to *Merriam-Webster's Collegiate Dictionary*, *cope* means "to deal with and attempt to overcome problems and difficulties."

When we can no longer cope with our lives, we feel we've lost control. We are drowning in our lives' problems. How could we possibly say, with the apostle Paul in this scripture passage, that we are content with these circumstances?

Paul's life was far from easy; he faced prison, shipwreck, persecution, and criticism from all sides. If anyone had the right to throw up his hands and say, "I can't cope any longer!" it was him. And yet despite all these problems in his life, he claimed he had learned to be contented in every situation, whether good or bad.

What was Paul's secret? Perhaps he had learned a new definition of *coping*. He knew that he could rely on God's strength to deal with and overcome each and every challenge he faced.

PRAY:
When I've reached the end of my power to cope, remind me, Lord, that You will help me do all things through Your strength.

I'M FULL OF ENVY

READ PROVERBS 14:26–30

KEY VERSE:
*A sound heart is the life of the flesh:
but envy the rottenness of the bones.*
PROVERBS 14:30 KJV

UNDERSTAND:

- What do you think is meant by a "sound heart"?
- How might envy rot the "bones" of your being?
- Verse 29 (KJV) speaks of a "hasty spirit." What do those words convey to you? How might you apply them to your own life?

APPLY:

Envy and jealousy are often confused, and their meanings are similar. *Jealousy*, however, means we are afraid someone is a threat to something (or someone) we consider to be ours, while *envy* has to do with coveting something that someone else has, something that we lack. The wise author of Proverbs tells us that envy is a destructive emotion that can rot us to the core. According to author Neel Burton, in a 2014 article in *Psychology Today*, over time, envy "can lead to physical health problems such as infections, cardiovascular diseases, and cancers; and mental health problems such as depression, anxiety, and insomnia. We are, quite literally, consumed by envy."

In other words, we might say that envy leads to death. Trust in God (the knowledge that He will give us everything we need) leads in the exact opposite direction. In fact, it's a fountain of life!

PRAY:
Give me greater confidence in You, Lord, so that I will realize I have no need to envy anyone. After all, You give me everything I need.

THIS SITUATION TERRIFIES ME

READ PSALM 56:9–13

KEY VERSE:
I trust in God, so why should I be afraid?
What can mere mortals do to me?
PSALM 56:11 NLT

UNDERSTAND:

- Do you feel that God is truly on your side? Why or why not?
- When you look back at your life, can you recognize any places where God "kept [your] feet from slipping" (verse 13 NLT)? Does that diminish your fears about the current situation?

APPLY:

Life is scary! Dangers are everywhere. Every day we face emotional, physical, and spiritual threats. If we think about our fears too much, it's enough to make us want to curl up in our beds and never venture out into the world!

The psalmist, however, described a way of life that is confident, courageous, and joyful. He affirmed that God is on his side, but he also reminded himself that this is a reciprocal relationship; God can only keep His promises to us when we surrender our lives into His keeping. If we keep yanking them back, trying to take control, we stand in God's way. He's longing to rush to our aid, but in effect, we're refusing to let Him. No wonder we're terrified!

PRAY:
Help me, Savior, to trust You and only You. When I walk in Your presence, I know I can rely on You to protect me from every enemy. You're on my side!

I'M HOMESICK

READ JOHN 15:9–11

KEY VERSE:
"Make yourselves at home in my love.
If you keep my commands, you'll remain
intimately at home in my love."
JOHN 15:9 MSG

UNDERSTAND:

- What do you think is so painful about being homesick? In other words, what is it that you miss most (comfort, companionship, familiarity)?
- Have you ever had the feeling of being homesick—and yet known that there's no actual geographical location you can call home?
- During His time on earth, do you think Jesus ever felt homesick for His home in heaven?

APPLY:

Even the most adventurous soul needs a home to return to at the end of all the excitement. Home is where our bodies, minds, and spirits are restored. It's the place where we can let down our defenses. We can relax and simply be ourselves.

When we're separated from our homes for too long, we feel sick at heart. We may even begin to feel physically ill. We grow weary of unfamiliar beds, unfamiliar foods, and unfamiliar faces; we long to *go home*!

In this Gospel passage, Jesus tells us that He wants to give us a portable home, one that we can carry with us wherever we go. That home is His love. When we keep His commands (to love God and to love one another), then we can experience the intimate, familiar comfort of being at home.

PRAY:
Jesus, I want my home to be Your love. Whenever I travel away from that home, make me so homesick that I run quickly back to You.

I FEEL REJECTED

READ JOHN 15:18–27

KEY VERSE:
*"If the world hates you,
remember that it hated me first."*
JOHN 15:18 NLT

UNDERSTAND:

- Have you ever considered how rejected Jesus must have felt when He hung on the cross? He was rejected not only by humanity but even by His heavenly Father.
- How do you think the Holy Spirit might help you face the pain of rejection?

APPLY:

The Greek word in this Gospel passage that has been translated "world" refers to the entire system of reality in which we live—the physical world, human society, the invisible spiritual world. . .the whole kit and caboodle. So when Jesus says that the world hated Him, He's saying that all of reality rejected its own Creator.

No rejection we experience will ever be as immense or total as that, and yet Jesus isn't saying to us, "You think *you've* got it bad—look at what *I* had to go through!" No, instead He's saying, "I know how rejection feels. But the rejection I experienced wasn't deserved, and neither is yours. What's more, I love you so much, I don't want you to have to face rejection alone. That's why I'm sending the Spirit to you. Even though I can't be with you now in physical form, the Spirit will tell you about Me—so that you can tell others."

PRAY:
Jesus, I am so sorry that You had to endure the world's rejection. Help me to face the smaller rejections in my own life with Your Spirit of love and gentleness.

MY FRIEND ANNOYS ME

READ 1 THESSALONIANS 5:15–24

KEY VERSE:
*Make sure that nobody pays back
wrong for wrong, but always strive
to do what is good for each other.*
1 THESSALONIANS 5:15 NIV

UNDERSTAND:
- What is it about your friend that annoys you so much? Can you get to the bottom of what's *really* bothering you?
- Do you think your annoyance might "quench" the Spirit's presence in your life (verse 19 NIV)? If so, why might that happen?
- Verse 23 (NIV) speaks of God sanctifying you "through and through." What does that mean to you?

APPLY:
Even the closest friends can grate on our nerves. Maybe it's the way they eat. . .or talk . . .or behave. Maybe it's simply that their careless words and actions hurt our feelings. Our

annoyance can mushroom, expanding larger and larger until we dread being with these individuals. We stop caring very much about what they may need from us, and instead, we focus on how much they bug us. If we keep going in this direction, we may find that we've killed the friendship altogether.

God calls us to turn around before we reach that point. Instead of paying back wrong for wrong, He challenges us to focus on ways we can be of help to our friends. He asks us to pray for them, to rejoice in their unique personalities, and to give thanks for them. And then He promises that He will be the One who will do all this for us, through us.

PRAY:
Jesus, I pray for my friend who annoys me. Remind me of what drew me to this person in the first place. Help me to focus more on my friend and her needs than I do on my irritation. Keep me blameless, spirit, soul, and body, so that my life is an expression of Your ever-faithful friendship.

I'M SUCH A COWARD!

READ 2 TIMOTHY 1:1–7

KEY VERSE:
For God has not given us a spirit of fear and timidity, but of power, love, and self-discipline.
2 TIMOTHY 1:7 NLT

UNDERSTAND:

- Can you describe the sort of relationship that Paul had with Timothy, based on this passage from Paul's letter?
- Based on Paul's advice, can you imagine what problems Timothy might have been facing?
- How would you feel if you were to receive this letter from someone you admire and respect?

APPLY:
In this passage of Paul's letter to a young friend, we get a sense of the intimacy between these two men. Paul placed his words within the context of both his own ancestors (verse 3) and Timothy's grandmother and mother (verse 5). In doing so, perhaps he was reminding

Timothy that none of us stands alone; we are each linked by faith to all who have gone before us. When we feel cowardly, unable to face life's challenges, we can lay claim to this strong chain of faith. As we remember the strength and endurance of those whose lives contributed to our own, we will fan into flame the little sparks of courage we possess.

This takes self-discipline. And yet we don't have to pull ourselves up by our own boot-straps! Paul promised that God will give us the power and love we need to discipline ourselves—so that we can serve Him fearlessly.

PRAY:
God of power, I know Your Spirit is the opposite of timidity and fear. You are love—and love always dares to take action. Love is never a coward. Fill me with Your love.

I CAN'T BEAR CRITICISM

READ PROVERBS 15:31–33

KEY VERSE:
*Whoever heeds life-giving correction
will be at home among the wise.*
PROVERBS 15:31 NIV

UNDERSTAND:
- Can you describe the difference between "life-giving correction" and criticism that is merely cruel and destructive? Have you experienced both kinds of criticism? Do they hurt equally? Why or why not?
- Why do you think this scripture tells us that if we refuse to listen to helpful criticism, we actually despise ourselves (verse 32)?

APPLY:
Even well-intentioned criticism, given by people who genuinely love us and have our best interests at heart, can be painful to bear. It strikes at our sense of pride and crushes our sense of who we are.

But imagine you're dressed up to go to an important formal event. Unbeknownst to you, the back of your suit has an enormous stain on it. You can't see the stain, though, so you believe you're looking mighty fine. You're about to go out the door with your head held high, when a friend calls you back. "Honey," the friend says, "you'd better head right back upstairs and change your clothes. That suit has a big stain all over your backside."

Would you be angry with your friend for telling you the truth? So certain of yourself that you'd head on out the door, stain and all? Or would you be grateful?

PRAY:
Heavenly Friend, You know how much criticism hurts my heart. It knocks the little self-confidence I have right out from under me. Help me to understand, though, that I need others' honest perspectives to see my blind spots. I want to be the best version of myself, the self You created me to be.

I'M STRUGGLING WITH HATRED

READ LUKE 6:27–36

KEY VERSE:

*"Love your enemies, and do good, and lend,
expecting nothing in return; and your reward will
be great, and you will be sons of the Most High;
for He Himself is kind to ungrateful and evil men."*
LUKE 6:35 NASB

UNDERSTAND:

- Who are the people in your life you consider to be enemies? Be honest with yourself. Even though you might never label these individuals as enemies, your actions and attitudes may say something different.
- What does it mean to be merciful? Can you list three people you know to whom you might extend mercy today?

APPLY:

Sometimes we forget how radical Jesus' message truly is. It turns upside down the way we're accustomed to thinking about things. This passage from the Gospel of Luke is an example of how challenging Jesus can be to our habits and attitudes.

No matter how "Christian" we are, most of us feel justified in holding ourselves apart from those who are unkind to us. Doing so seems like a sensible stance to take. We may extend this attitude even further to those who disagree with us, politically or theologically. Why, we may ask ourselves, would God want us to associate with those who are clearly *wrong*?

Jesus' answer is clear. He couldn't care less about right and wrong; if that were the case, He would never have given His life for us. And He expects us to follow His example, loving others, even the unlovable, with no expectation of love returned.

PRAY:
Jesus, I ask Your help today to act in love to everyone, even those who have mistreated me. May I carry Your Spirit out into the world.

I NEED HUMILITY

READ JAMES 4:6–10

KEY VERSE:
*"GOD is opposed to the proud,
but gives grace to the humble."*
JAMES 4:6 NASB

UNDERSTAND:

- What does the word *grace* convey to you?
- How do you think pride might act as a wall between you and God?
- Notice the effect of pride in your life. What feels good about pride? What aspects of pride have turned hurtful for you?

APPLY:

There's a healthy kind of pride, a sense of God-given dignity that is the birthright of each of us—but that's not the sort of pride that this scripture is talking about. The word translated as "proud" was a Greek word that meant, literally, to think of oneself as better than others. *Humble*, on the other hand, meant someone willing to take a lower position. HELPS Word-Studies defines *scriptural humility* as "being God-reliant rather than self-reliant." When we rely on God rather than ourselves, we have humility.

Selfish, egotistical pride can form a hard shell around our hearts. Sometimes it takes the tears of genuine sorrow to wash it away. Then when we finally come into God's presence, naked, low, with no more pretense, He will lift us up.

PRAY:
God, my proud heart needs Your grace. Wash me with humble tears. I want to come closer to You.

BITTERNESS IS EATING ME UP

READ HEBREWS 12:14–25

KEY VERSE:
*See to it that no one falls short of the grace
of God and that no bitter root grows up
to cause trouble and defile many.*
HEBREWS 12:15 NIV

UNDERSTAND:

- What in your life today is leaving a bitter taste in your mouth?
- Notice that verse 17 indicates that sometimes, even though our hearts change, we cannot avoid the consequences of our earlier bitterness. Have you ever experienced this?

APPLY:

Bitterness may start out as anger, hurt, disappointment, frustration, or resentment. It takes root when we refuse to let go of these other emotions, holding them tight until they turn into something cold, hard, and habitual.

No matter how bitterness starts out, this scripture tells us that it can end up causing all sorts of trouble. It can spread from us to others, weakening the body of Christ. It can lead to other forms of brokenness. Worst of all, it will come between our hearts and God's.

"You have no reason to be bitter," God says to us in these verses. "You're no longer living in the Old Testament world, where I was so often perceived as angry and terrifying. Instead, I've invited you to be a part of the angels' joyful gathering. I've erased the bitter blood Cain spilled when he murdered his brother—and I've sprinkled you with the love of My own Son."

PRAY:
God of love, I ask that You show me how to pull out any roots of bitterness in my heart. Help me to hear Your voice more clearly so that I can live in Your joy.

MY IMPULSIVENESS HAS GOTTEN ME IN TROUBLE— AGAIN!

READ 1 THESSALONIANS 5:4–8

KEY VERSE:
Let's keep our eyes open and be smart.
1 THESSALONIANS 5:6 MSG

UNDERSTAND:
- Can you identify what is at the root of your impulsiveness? Is it pride. . . genuine concern for others. . .or just sheer carelessness?
- *The Message* version of these verses says that since we are "sons of Light" and "daughters of Day" we live under "wide open skies" (verse 5). What images do these words shape in your mind? How might you use them to remind you to think more carefully the next time your impulsiveness threatens to lead you astray?

APPLY:
"I didn't mean any harm," we sometimes say.

"I just acted impulsively." We seem to assume that our failure to think carefully about our behavior will excuse any hurtful consequences of our actions. Deep down, though, doesn't acting impulsively imply that we think we can do whatever we want? Even if we say we were motivated by love or kindness or pure excitement, acting without thinking is selfish. It can cause great damage to ourselves and others.

We're not walking through life asleep or inebriated, our senses inoperative or dulled. God gave us brains, expecting us to make use of them. He doesn't want us stumbling around in the dark, following every whim that crosses our minds. Instead, He wants us to walk carefully, soberly, clothed in His love.

Pray:
Lord, forgive me for acting so impulsively yet again. Teach me to discipline myself so that I always take time to think before I act. Strip me of my headstrong pride so that You can dress me in faith, love, and the hope of Your salvation.

MY HEART IS BROKEN

READ PSALM 34:15–20

KEY VERSE:
The LORD is near to the brokenhearted
and saves those who are crushed in spirit.
PSALM 34:18 NASB

UNDERSTAND:

- What has broken your heart? Was it the betrayal of someone you trusted? Or the death of a loved one? In both cases, you have experienced a serious loss.
- Notice the way this psalm connects emotional injury to physical pain. Can you feel your broken heart in your body? Where does the pain settle—in your stomach, your chest, your head?

APPLY:
A broken heart can shatter our sense of who we are. It may even make us doubt God and His promises. We feel as though the very bones of our lives, the structures that held them together, have been smashed, leaving us unable to walk away from this terrible pain.

The psalmist tells us, however, that as much as a broken heart hurts, God will not let it destroy us. God is like a mother who hears her child sobbing in the night and immediately gets up to offer love and comfort. The pain will not immediately lift from our hearts—but we can be certain that God is with us, holding us tight, rocking us in His loving arms.

And one day, we will find that the vital bones that held us up were not broken after all. Thanks to God's tender care, we will be able to walk again.

PRAY:
Be near to me, Lord. I need You desperately. Don't leave me alone with this terrible pain. Hold me in Your arms and mend my broken heart.

MY HEART IS POUNDING WITH FEAR

READ 1 CHRONICLES 28:11–20

KEY VERSE:
"Be strong and courageous, and do the work. Don't be afraid or discouraged, for the LORD God, my God, is with you. He will not fail you or forsake you."
1 CHRONICLES 28:20 NLT

UNDERSTAND:

- Notice the details that are included in this scripture passage regarding the exact specifications for the temple (verses 11–19). Do you think it's just coincidence that these verses were included directly before the key verse? Do you see any connection between such practical directions and the courage that David described in verse 20? Why or why not?
- How does fear interfere with your ability to do the work to which God has called you?

APPLY:

Fear makes our hearts pound and our breath come fast. Our stomachs feel sick, and our hands turn cold. These reactions are intended to prepare our bodies to either fight danger or run away from it. In that sense, fear is healthy. It can be our friend.

Often, however, particularly in the modern world, neither fight nor flight is an option. When that's the case, fear is no friend. Instead, it can interfere with our ability to do the work God wants us to do. We may find ourselves confused, getting in even worse trouble as we run back and forth like a frantic rabbit. *If only God would give us precise directions*, we may think to ourselves, *like He gave His people when they were building the temple.*

But He has! His Word, the Bible, contains His directions written in His own hand. It can keep us on course, no matter how scared we are.

PRAY:

Give me the strength and courage I need, God, to be of use to You and Your kingdom. Don't let me be so fearful that I become too discouraged to keep going. Remind me that You are always with me.

MY FEELINGS ARE CONFLICTED

READ PSALM 32:8–11

KEY VERSE:
"I will guide you along the best pathway for your life. I will advise you and watch over you."
PSALM 32:8 NLT

UNDERSTAND:
- What creates the conflict in your heart? What is it that pulls you in opposite directions?
- These verses imply that joy and praise are directly related to a greater sense of clear direction. Have you ever found that to be true? Can you try it out today to see if it helps you think more clearly?

APPLY:
We often feel pulled in opposite directions, like poor Olive Oyl stretched between Popeye and Brutus. Should we do what our hearts call us to do? Or should we be "responsible" and take the safer course? When is it smart to be conservative about money—and when should we be extravagant and generous? What's the

difference between giving our children too much freedom and being overprotective? How do we determine when frankness is cruel—and when it's necessary and kind?

Life is so confusing! But God promises to guide us. When we turn to Him, relying only on Him, things become more clear. We can live in the stream of His unfailing love, trusting Him to resolve the conflicts in our hearts.

PRAY:
I praise You, loving Lord, for all You are and do. Keep my heart whole and pure, free of the conflicts that drive me back and forth. Show me the best path to take.

I'M PANICKED

READ PSALM 91

KEY VERSE:
This I declare about the LORD:
He alone is my refuge, my place of
safety; he is my God, and I trust him.
PSALM 91:2 NLT

UNDERSTAND:
- How do you think panic is different from other kinds of fear? What in your life makes you panic?
- How might scripture be the antidote for panic's poison? Consider writing some of the verses in this passage of scripture on a note card or in your phone, somewhere you can refer to them whenever panic threatens to overcome you.

APPLY:
The original meaning of *panic*, dating back a few hundred years, had to do with the sort of contagious, unreasoning fear that can sweep through a herd of cattle—or a crowd of people—causing them to run into even worse danger.

In fact, the original thing that triggers panic is often not even an actual danger; it might be merely a sudden loud sound or an event that startles us. Panic can be personal, but it can also sweep through an entire society, creating a state of fear that's so overpowering, we lose our ability to think clearly.

Panic is destructive—but we don't have to let it control our lives. Instead, as soon as we notice panic's poisonous touch, we can turn immediately to the only One who can hold us steady. He is our refuge, our place of safety. We can rest in His shadow.

PRAY:
Cover me with Your feathers, almighty God. Shield me with Your wings. Protect me with the armor of Your faithfulness. When panic threatens to grab me in its grasp, remind me that You are with me, saving me from every danger—including the ones that exist only in my imagination!

I FEEL SO LOST!

READ LUKE 15:4–7

KEY VERSE:
"When he has found it, he lays it on his shoulders, rejoicing. And when he comes home, he calls together his friends and his neighbors, saying to them, 'Rejoice with me, for I have found my sheep which was lost!'"
LUKE 15:5–6 NASB

UNDERSTAND:
- Feeling lost can be caused by a variety of circumstances. What is making you feel lost?
- Can you imagine yourself as a lost sheep—and picture God as a Shepherd who will never stop searching for you until you are safe in His arms?
- Do you think we are ever *really* lost to God?

APPLY:
In the Gospels, Jesus tells three little stories that are all similar. In this story, a shepherd searches for a lost sheep. In another story,

a woman searches her house for a lost coin until she finds it, and then she shares her joy with her friends. In the third story, a man's son runs away from home—and then comes home at last, where he is greeted with love and celebration. In each of these stories, where God is represented by a shepherd, a housewife, and a father, Jesus never implies that God blames the lost one for going astray. And He makes it clear that the joy of being found is one that's shared throughout the entire kingdom of God.

When we feel lost, we can rest in the assurance that God is searching for us. He will find us, and when He does, even the angels will rejoice.

PRAY:
Thank You, Jesus, that You do not blame me for all the ways I lose myself. I am so grateful I can trust You to bring me back home.

MY ACHES AND PAINS
MAKE ME MISERABLE

READ PROVERBS 17:22–24

KEY VERSE:
A cheerful heart is good medicine,
but a crushed spirit dries up the bones.
PROVERBS 17:22 NIV

UNDERSTAND:

- Have you ever noticed a connection between your emotions and your physical pain? Certainly, pain can make us emotionally depressed—but do you think a gloomy attitude can make our pain seem more severe? Why or why not?
- Do you see any connection between verse 22 and the two verses that follow it? What might that connection be?

APPLY:

We often think of our bodies as being separate from our minds and souls. We look at physical pain as a burden we must shoulder emotionally and spiritually, which in one sense it is. In another sense, as both the Bible and modern science make clear, we cannot divide ourselves into pieces. What is good for our bodies is good for our hearts and souls—and what is bad for our hearts and souls can also damage our bodies. If we are wise and discerning, we'll stop looking here and there for something to take away our misery—and instead take time to search ourselves for a spiritual root to our physical pain.

It's hard to be in a good mood when our bodies are in pain, and not every physical condition can be healed. Choosing to be cheerful rather than complaining, however, could be just the medicine God wants us to take!

PRAY:
God, You know how hard it is to be cheerful when every movement makes me hurt. This pain makes me cross and cranky. Give me the courage to accept Your will for my life, whatever it is. Make me wise enough to choose Your joy, even in the midst of my misery.

MY MOODS OVERWHELM ME

READ ECCLESIASTES 3:1–8

KEY VERSE:
*To every thing there is a season, and a time
to every purpose under the heaven: . . .
a time to weep, and a time to laugh;
a time to mourn, and a time to dance.*
ECCLESIASTES 3:1, 4 KJV

UNDERSTAND:
- What does this passage of scripture say to you about the interplay between positive and negative emotions in our lives?
- Do you feel guilty for having certain negative emotions? Why or why not?

APPLY:
Somehow, we've gotten the impression that strong people don't experience strong emotions. The Bible never tells us that. The great heroes of the faith, including Jesus, experienced boisterous moods. They were swept with rage, they wept with sorrow, they danced with joy, and they shouted with laughter.

There's nothing wrong with having moods! In fact, since they're a part of normal human life, it's safe to say that they're a gift from God, one He intended to enrich our lives. That doesn't mean, of course, that we should let our moods have more power over us than God does or that we should allow them to rob us of our confidence in His love. But as this scripture tells us, there is a time and place for everything. Each season of our lives—each circumstance and each emotion we feel in response—can teach us something about ourselves and the God who loves us.

PRAY:
Lord of both joy and sorrow, remind me that You created my emotions. I pray that my moods might not control me—but that they will give You glory.

THIS SECRET IS DESTROYING ME

READ HEBREWS 4:12–16

KEY VERSE:
*Nothing in all creation is hidden from
God's sight. Everything is uncovered
and laid bare before the eyes of him
to whom we must give account.*
HEBREWS 4:13 NIV

UNDERSTAND:

- Why do you keep secrets from others (and from God, maybe even from yourself)? Can you identify what motivates you? Is it shame, pride—or something else?
- Do you find it comforting or frightening to be reminded that you can't hide from God?
- What would it cost you to reveal this secret? Do you think it would bring healing—or cause more damage?

APPLY:

Old things that are left to rot in the dark have a way of seeping into the rest of our life. "Out of sight, out of mind" does not mean powerless! Secrets can be a potent and deadly poison.

We may be hiding the truth out of shame or guilt (which are two different things). Many of us carry within us the secret of either sexual abuse or sexual sin. As terrifying as it may seem to reveal a secret like that, it may be the only way for us to truly heal. What looms in the darkness may prove to be more manageable once it's out in the light of day.

These verses of scripture remind us that nothing is hidden from God. No matter what secrets we are keeping, whether our own or someone else's, He knows all about it—and He longs to lift its weight from our hearts.

PRAY:
Thank You, Jesus, that You understand my every weakness. Give me the courage and discernment to know what to do with this terrible secret I've been hiding. I put it in Your hands.

I LACK SELF-CONFIDENCE

READ 2 CORINTHIANS 10:12–18

KEY VERSE:
We do not dare to classify or compare ourselves with some who commend themselves. When they measure themselves by themselves and compare themselves with themselves, they are not wise. We, however, will not boast beyond proper limits, but will confine our boasting to the sphere of service God himself has assigned to us.
2 CORINTHIANS 10:12–13 NIV

UNDERSTAND:

- How much of your lack of confidence comes from comparing yourself to others?
- Do you feel guilty or embarrassed to identify your own unique abilities? Why?
- What attitude do you think God wants you to take toward the skills and talents He has given you?

APPLY:
Self-confidence is a necessary aspect of being

a healthy, productive human being. Without it, we will be afraid to do the work God has called us to do. And yet often, especially as Christians, we are afraid to lay claim to our own strength. We confuse self-confidence with egotistical pride.

In this passage of scripture, written by Paul to the church at Corinth, the apostle makes it clear that there's an enormous difference between selfish, prideful boasting and the humble acknowledgment of skills God has given us to use in His service. To pretend that we have not each been given unique abilities would be like a carpenter who was given a hammer but refused—out of a sense of modesty—to put it to use. God wants us to pick up our abilities and use them confidently to build His kingdom.

PRAY:

Thank You, God of grace, that You have given me the skills that I possess. Don't let my lack of self-confidence prevent me from seeing clearly what You have given me, so that I can offer it back in service to You.

I'M MY OWN WORST CRITIC

READ PSALM 55:16–22

KEY VERSE:
*As for me, I will call upon God;
and the LORD shall save me.*
PSALM 55:16 KJV

UNDERSTAND:
- This psalm speaks of an exterior battle—but often the fiercest battles are waged within our hearts. In what ways do you attack your own self?
- What do you hate most about yourself? Can you give it to God, believing that He can truly sustain you (verse 22)?

APPLY:
Self-criticism is like a sharp sword that attacks our inner strength. It destroys the peace God wants us to experience. It can even make us believe that God has broken His promises to us. Self-criticism may seem like modesty or humility—but it's actually a demonic attack on all God has given us.

We need to treat those inner voices that

tell us we're unworthy with the discipline they deserve. Sometimes, though, our strength is too weak to stand up to the whispers that slide like oil into our minds. When that happens, we need to turn immediately to God and call for help. He has the strength to carry us through this inner battle. His love will hold us firm.

Pray:
Dear Lord, I'm calling on You for help. The enemy I face is inside my own heart, and I don't know how to fight it. Save me!

I FEEL LIKE HURTING MYSELF

READ 1 CORINTHIANS 6:19–20

KEY VERSE:
*What? know ye not that your body is the
temple of the Holy Ghost which is in you,
which ye have of God, and ye are not your own?*
1 CORINTHIANS 6:19 KJV

UNDERSTAND:
- Have you ever (or do you now) hurt your body intentionally? If so, can you identify what drives you to do this?
- How do you think God feels if you hurt yourself? Does it make Him angry with you—or does it cause Him pain?

APPLY:
Self-harm is one of the more deadly secrets we may hide from others' view. It can take many forms—from cutting ourselves to abusing drugs or alcohol, from overeating to starving ourselves—but whatever its form, it's usually a way we handle a very deep psychological pain.

Healing a self-harm habit is not easy or

simple, and those of us who have this secret are likely to need professional help. Taking that first step and seeking help can be the hardest one of all. Perhaps if we remind ourselves that our bodies are the Spirit's temple, bought by the blood of Jesus, then we will find the courage we need.

God loves us so much, and His love encompasses our bodies, our wounded hearts, and our glorious spirits. He longs to set us free from the self-hatred that drives us to hurt our own flesh. He wants us to be healed.

Pray:
Jesus, I'm so ashamed of this habit of mine that I hate to admit it even to myself. I keep it in its secret compartment, bringing it out only when I feel I need it. It's been with me so long that I feel helpless to fight it. Help me! I want to glorify You with my entire being—body, heart, and spirit.

MY PAST IS
WEIGHING ME DOWN

READ 2 CORINTHIANS 5:17–19

KEY VERSE:
*Anyone united with the Messiah gets
a fresh start, is created new. The old
life is gone; a new life burgeons!*
2 CORINTHIANS 5:17 MSG

UNDERSTAND:
- Can you see ways in which your past is weighing down your present?
- Do you feel that the past is truly gone? Or do you still feel it haunting you, standing in the way of your growth?

APPLY:
The Bible's message is truly good news! Rather than being a message of doom and gloom, don't-do-this and don't-do-that, it's full of joy and hope. These verses are wonderful expressions of God's vision for us.

The old life, with all its pain and shame and brokenness, need hold us back no longer. Through Jesus the Messiah (the One anointed by God), we are born anew. We have a fresh start. We can leave the past behind and experience a new relationship both with God and with other human beings.

In the words of *The Message*, "The old life is gone; a new life burgeons!"

P<small>RAY</small>:
Jesus, thank You for the new life You've given me in You. Help me to step away from my past, with all its destructive habits, behaviors, and attitudes. Make me into a new creature, one who grows more like You with each day we share together.

WHY DO I SABOTAGE MYSELF?

READ ROMANS 8:1–17

KEY VERSE:
So letting your sinful nature control your mind leads to death. But letting the Spirit control your mind leads to life and peace.
ROMANS 8:6 NLT

UNDERSTAND:
- Can you identify specific ways that you have sabotaged yourself in the past year?
- What do you think motivates your acts of self-sabotage? Is it fear. . . self-hatred. . .shame. . .or something else? Discussing this issue with someone whose discernment and love you trust may be helpful.

APPLY:
Self-sabotage makes no rational sense—Why would we prevent ourselves from achieving our goals?—and yet most of us have committed this act of self-betrayal at one time or another. We may not be able to see these actions

immediately, but we'd be wise to take a closer look. If we can identify behaviors that have led us over and over down the wrong paths, we're probably sabotaging our own growth. This might take the form of getting involved again and again in destructive relationships, or it might show up as a repeated tendency to hesitate at the crucial moment, causing us to lose out on life-giving opportunities.

Whatever form it takes, it's a form of unconscious sin that leads to death rather than the life God wants us to experience. But we don't have to be a slave to it any longer. Jesus has freed us, and His Spirit can lead us down new paths.

PRAY:
Holy Spirit, reveal to me the ways I sabotage myself. I don't want to lie to myself any longer. Give me the courage to become the person You created me to be.

I WISH I HAD MORE MONEY!

READ HEBREWS 13:5–8

KEY VERSE:
*Don't love money; be satisfied with
what you have. For God has said, "I will
never fail you. I will never abandon you."*
HEBREWS 13:5 NLT

UNDERSTAND:

- Do you think your longing for more money could be something that comes between you and God? Why or why not?
- What connection, if any, do you think your longing for money has with a lack of trust in God?
- Why do you think this passage ends with the reminder that Jesus is the same yesterday, today, and forever (verse 8)? Does this have anything at all to do with money? If so, what?

APPLY:

The longing for more money is one many of us share. No matter how much money we actually have, it never seems to be enough. There's always more we wish we could do or have. . .if only we had the money!

We often forget that money isn't anything *real*. It's merely a handy tool that human beings have come up with to symbolize the value of work and objects. In and of itself, it's just paper and metal. And yet, we've allowed it to carry so much—our sense of our own worth, our longing for power and prestige, and our feelings that if we only had *more*, we could fill up the deep emptiness within our hearts. We think that somehow money can keep us safe from life's dangers.

Only God can do that. He knows what we need, and He will give us exactly enough. We can trust Him.

PRAY:
Jesus, money comes and goes, but You always stay the same. You are my only constant source of security. Teach me to rely only on You.

I KNOW I'M BEING SELFISH

READ PHILIPPIANS 2:4–9

KEY VERSE:
*You must have the same
attitude that Christ Jesus had.*
PHILIPPIANS 2:5 NLT

UNDERSTAND:

- Imagine if Jesus had been a "normal," selfish human being. How do you think His life would have been changed?
- Do you consider Jesus to be your role model? Why or why not?
- What do you think the world would look like if imitating Jesus became a shared societal norm?

APPLY:

Selfishness makes us want to impress other people with our skills, appearance, prestige, or some other quality, while it blinds us to the reality of others' needs. It makes us think, deep in our hearts, that we're somehow better than others. It drives us to seek our own way, regardless of the hurt it causes others.

Selfishness is woven through the very fabric of our society. As a result, it seems normal to us. Meanwhile, as it hurts our relationships at the individual level, at the societal level, it has polluted our planet, created wars and poverty, and driven us to prejudice, discrimination, and divisive factions of one sort or another.

We can't change our entire society, not without a great deal of concerted effort, but we *can* take the first, most vital step—we can allow God to change our own hearts. We can practice the attitudes of Christ.

PRAY:
Jesus, teach me to follow You more closely. Change our world, Lord, I pray—but first, change me. Remake me in Your image. I want to be like You.

I WANT TO HAVE MY OWN WAY!

READ 1 PETER 4:1–8

KEY VERSE:
Since Jesus went through everything you're going through and more, learn to think like him. Think of your sufferings as a weaning from that old sinful habit of always expecting to get your own way.
1 PETER 4:1 MSG

UNDERSTAND:

- In what areas of your life is it hardest for you to give up your own way?
- When you don't get your way, does it cause you pain? How might this pain be put to spiritual use, allowing you to become more like Jesus?

APPLY:

From the time we were babies, we've been crying and frustrated every time we couldn't get our own way. As we've grown older, we may have learned to disguise this better. We may have figured out other ways aside from yelling and having a tantrum to get what we want, but we still really want what we want!

Even Jesus struggled with this. That's why He prayed in the garden, sweating drops of blood as He begged His Father to find another path for Him to take, one that didn't lead to the cross. And yet, regardless of His natural longing to escape suffering and death, again and again He placed the entire situation back in His Father's hands. "Not My will," He said, "but only Yours."

Do we have the courage to follow His example?

PRAY:
Free me, Jesus, from the tyranny of my selfishness. Wean me from the babyish habit of wanting my own way. Keep me wide awake and alert to the Spirit, as You were when You prayed in the garden.

I AM THINKING ABOUT SUICIDE

READ 1 KINGS 19:3–9

KEY VERSE:
The angel of the LORD came back a second time and touched him and said, "Get up and eat, for the journey is too much for you."
1 KINGS 19:7 NIV

UNDERSTAND:

- If you're considering suicide, you need to tell someone. This is a problem that's too big for you to handle on your own. Regular Bible study and prayer can begin the process that will heal your heart—but God uses other human beings, often trained professionals, to deal directly with serious issues like these. Get help now.

- When thoughts of suicide haunt you, do these thoughts spring from shame, fear, depression, exhaustion. . .or a combination of all these? Can you offer this pain up to God?

APPLY:

Even Elijah, the great prophet, became so discouraged, he wanted to die. He was afraid, lonely, exhausted, unable to think clearly about his life. When God sent His angel to help Elijah, notice that the angel didn't deliver some enormous, miraculous solution to all of Elijah's problems. Instead, the angel did something small and practical: he gave Elijah something to eat and drink.

When we find ourselves ready to give up on life, we need to remember that we're not facing an either-or choice between death and finding an immediate, absolute solution to our despair. Doing just one small thing, right now, that will strengthen us—such as eating something, going for a walk, talking to a friend, or even taking a nap—may make things look just a little different. Afterward, our desolation may not be as absolute. It may have lifted enough that we can catch a glimpse of how precious our life is to God.

PRAY:

God, You know the despair I'm feeling. Life no longer seems worth living. I can't fix this problem on my own. Show me whom to talk to, and give me the courage to confess my suicidal feelings. I have no strength left of my own. Help me.

I FEEL SHY

READ EXODUS 4:1–12

KEY VERSE:
*"I will be with you as you speak,
and I will instruct you in what to say."*
EXODUS 4:12 NLT

UNDERSTAND:

- How does being shy hold you back from doing God's work?
- What "staff" might God have given you (verse 2) that He wants to use in some miraculous way you've never imagined? Is there something you've been leaning on, psychologically, that God wants you to surrender to Him—so that He can transform it into something alive and amazing?

APPLY:

Moses, the great father of the Jewish and Christian faiths, allowed his shyness to get in God's way. He thought he could tell God, "Come on, Lord. You know I'm not good with words. I'm shy. I always have been. That's just the way I am." He seemed to think he knew more about his limitations and abilities than God, his Creator, did.

We often make the same mistake. We act as though shyness is an insurmountable barrier that prevents us from answering God's call on our lives. "Sorry, God," we say. "I'd really like to obey You—but I just can't. I'm too shy."

No wonder God gets exasperated (both with Moses and with us). "Who made your mouth?" He asks. "Who knows better than Me what you're capable of doing? Do you think I'd ask you to do something I knew was impossible for you to do?"

PRAY:
God, You know how my shyness gets in my way. I don't know how to overcome it—so I'm giving it to You. Shy or not, I'll go wherever You want, do whatever You ask, and say anything You tell me to say. Transform me into something You can use to build Your realm on earth.

I RESENT SOMEONE

READ MARK 11:22–25

KEY VERSE:
*"When you assume the posture of prayer,
remember that it's not all asking. If you
have anything against someone, forgive."*
MARK 11:25 MSG

UNDERSTAND:

- If you've allowed resentment to take root in your heart, have you noticed that it hinders your ability to pray? Are you able to come into God's presence with the same sense of intimacy you once had?
- In the words of *The Message*, Jesus asks us to "embrace this God-life" (verse 22). What does the term "God-life" convey to you? How might you embrace it?

APPLY:

"Help me with this, Lord," we pray. "Give me that. Do this; do that." We have so many directions for the Creator of the universe! And yet God loves to know we trust Him enough to bring our petitions to Him. Most of all, He simply loves to hear our voices.

But Jesus reminds us in these verses that prayer is more than asking God for something. We might think His next words will be a reminder to praise God—but no, Jesus turns our attention to our relationship with others. We can't be in an intimate relationship with God, He tells us, if we've put up walls between our hearts and another's.

Resentment is one of the highest walls we erect against the people in our lives. It's built out of the unwillingness to forgive. Ultimately, it will not only separate us from others; it will also separate us from God.

Time to tear down that wall!

PRAY:
Knock down the walls in my heart, loving Lord. Show me how to truly embrace the God-life You want to share with me.

I DON'T KNOW HOW TO SET HEALTHY BOUNDARIES

READ PSALM 16:1–8

KEY VERSE:
The boundary lines have fallen for me in pleasant places; surely I have a delightful inheritance.
PSALM 16:6 NIV

UNDERSTAND:
- If setting boundaries—such as saying no to someone's request—makes you uncomfortable, why do you think that is? Do you feel guilty if you don't do what others want? Do you think God expects that of you?
- How has your lack of boundaries hurt you? Can you examine your life to see how healthy boundaries would have protected you from unnecessary pain?
- What boundaries might God be calling you to put in place in your life? This is something to ponder and pray about.

APPLY:
Somehow, many of us have gotten confused

about the necessity of boundary lines. We assume that Christ's command to lay down our lives for others means we don't have the right to say no to others' requests. We seem to think that God expects us to let others trample over our time and energy, taking whatever they want.

But boundaries are necessary to our emotional, spiritual, and even physical health. They not only help us to keep danger out, but they also allow us to protect the resources we have within, including our relationship with God.

With God's guidance, we can learn to set the boundaries that will define the pleasant places where we can grow, the territory of Divine inheritance that will allow us to find safety and refuge. Then, when God calls us to venture out beyond these lines, we can act with strength, with all our God-given resources available for our use.

PRAY:
God, I need Your counsel. Teach me to listen to my own heart. Show me where I should say yes—and when I should say no. I need a safe space where I can be alone with You.

I WANT TO RUN AWAY

READ JONAH 1

KEY VERSE:
*But Jonah ran away from the LORD. . .
He went down to Joppa, where he found a ship
. . . After paying the fare, he went aboard and
sailed for Tarshish to flee from the LORD.*
JONAH 1:3 NIV

UNDERSTAND:
- Why do you think Jonah ran away from God? Why was he so unwilling to go to Nineveh?
- If you feel like running away from your life, have you considered that you may also be running away from God?

APPLY:
Sometimes we all need to run away. Even Jesus needed times of escape. But there's a big difference between running away *to God*, as Jesus did, and running away *from God*, as Jonah did.

Jonah's story shows us what happens when we try to escape God's will. Thinking we can flee whatever demands we're unwilling to face, we end up somewhere far worse! We're not likely to be swallowed by a giant fish, but any circumstances where we're cramped, in the dark, and miserable might be a lot like that whale's belly!

There's an interesting detail in this story, though—Jonah was in the fish's stomach for three days and nights (verse 17), the same period of time that Jesus was in the grave. This hints at something important: Even though we run away from God, all is not lost. God uses even the graves in our lives—the slimy, smelly, dark fish bellies—to transform us. He can resurrect us into a new life, a life aligned with His love.

PRAY:
God, when I want to run away, remind me what happened to Jonah. Thank You that even when I insist on fleeing from You, You give me another chance. You send a whale to swallow me—and then You bring me back to serve You anew.

NOTHING MAKES ANY SENSE

READ LUKE 1:26–38

KEY VERSE:
*"I am the Lord's servant. May everything
you have said about me come true."*
LUKE 1:38 NLT

UNDERSTAND:

- Can you imagine how Mary must have felt when she was confronted with an angel telling her that she was going to have a baby even though she was a virgin? If something like that happened to you, what would your response be? Would you be able to respond as Mary did?

- When you think of the bewildering, confusing aspects of your own life, can you imagine that God is using these events in some mysterious way to give new birth to His Spirit? What might that mean? Would you be willing to allow it to happen?

APPLY:
Comparing the confusion in our lives to Mary's

situation may seem inappropriate. But remember, Mary was only a simple young girl at the time the angel came to her. She had no idea how the story would end or the important role she would play. (She would have been astounded if she knew that one day many churches would portray her image!) At the time, she was completely and utterly bewildered. Nothing would have made sense to her.

And yet how did this teenage girl respond? With total surrender to whatever God wanted to do in her life!

PRAY:
Lord, I don't understand what You're doing in my life. Nothing makes sense to me. But I am Your servant. Accomplish whatever You want in my life. Be born in me.

I HAVE A PERMANENT CLOUD OVER MY HEAD

READ PSALM 30

KEY VERSE:
You have turned my mourning into joyful dancing. You have taken away my clothes of mourning and clothed me with joy.
PSALM 30:11 NLT

UNDERSTAND:

- Why is there a cloud over your head? What shape does it take? What brought it there?

- If you remember that clouds bring rain and rain brings new growth, can you bear more patiently with this cloud?

- If this cloud has been over your head for a very long time, with no sign of either moving or letting down its rain, you may need to seek professional help. Talk to your doctor, your minister, or a counselor. God can use these individuals to restore you to a happier, healthier frame of mind.

APPLY:

Depression can cast a cloud of gloom over our entire life. It can make it hard to see (or think) clearly. We feel as though God has abandoned us. We may think He is angry with us.

In reality, however, God has not gone anywhere, and nothing can change His love for us. He longs to lift us up above the clouds. He hears our cries, and He is already taking action to help us. Weeping may endure through the long, dark night—but a new joy will come with the rising of the sun (verse 5).

PRAY:

Hear me, Lord, and have mercy on me. Help me, Lord. Turn my mourning into joyful dancing. Take away my clothes of mourning and clothe me with joy, that I might sing praises to You and not be silent any longer. I will exalt You, Lord, for You rescued me. I cried to You for help, and You restored my health. You brought me up from the grave. You kept me from falling into the pit of death. I will give thanks to You forever! (See verses 10–12, 1–3 NLT.)

I'M NOT SURE GOD IS LISTENING

READ ISAIAH 58:1–59:2

KEY VERSE:
Listen! The LORD's arm is not too weak to save you, nor is his ear too deaf to hear you call.
ISAIAH 59:1 NLT

UNDERSTAND:

- When you read these verses, what strikes you?
- Can you see what came between God and His people?
- How can you apply this to your own life? Are you truly seeking God—or are you merely going through the motions?
- What does God expect of His people, according to these verses?

APPLY:

God's people felt that He wasn't hearing them. They believed they were living the way He wanted—going to church, praying, following all the rules—and yet they were allowing injustice to dwell in their midst.

God's message to them was loud and clear:

"I'm not the One who has gone deaf! I don't care how many times you go to church. What I really want is for you to free those who are wrongly imprisoned. Lighten the burden of those who work for you. Let the oppressed go free, and remove the chains that bind people. Share your food with the hungry, and give shelter to the homeless. Give clothes to those who need them, and do not hide from relatives who need your help. *That's* what I want from you!" (Isaiah 58:6–10).

PRAY:
God, thank You that You always hear my prayers. Teach me to hear You better. Show me how I can serve You in real and practical ways, reaching out to those who need my help.

I FEEL HELPLESS TO CONTROL THIS BAD HABIT

READ ROMANS 7:19–25

KEY VERSE:
For the good that I would I do not:
but the evil which I would not, that I do.
ROMANS 7:19 KJV

UNDERSTAND:
- How did this bad habit begin? Did you think it was something that would give you pleasure?
- Does this habit now seem like a dead body you're forced to carry on your shoulders (verse 24)?
- How does this habit keep you from living your life the way you want to live?
- If your habit is truly destructive—such as abusing drugs or harming yourself or others in some way—you need to seek help from outside yourself. Ask God to lead you to the professional help you need.

APPLY:
Haven't we all felt the way Paul did when he wrote these words? No matter how much we want to stop a certain behavior, we can't seem to shake it off. We make up our minds to never do this thing again—and then we turn around and do that very thing. It's so frustrating! We feel helpless and hopeless.

It may be that in our own power we're unable to break this habit. We need to understand, though, that God does not condemn us for the hold it has on our lives. If we surrender it to God, acknowledging that we are powerless to stop this behavior, God will be pleased. And as we trust Him, we may be surprised to find that He has brought people or circumstances into our lives we could never have imagined and which achieve what we thought could never be done: they set us free.

PRAY:
Lord, I ask that You deliver me from this bad habit. Show me the steps to take. Remind me that Your love for me is undiminished, no matter how powerless I am to control my own behavior.

I'M EMBARRASSED

READ 2 TIMOTHY 2:14–19

KEY VERSE:
*Be diligent to present yourself approved to God
as a workman who does not need to be ashamed,
accurately handling the word of truth.*
2 TIMOTHY 2:15 NASB

UNDERSTAND:

- What causes your embarrassment? Is it pride? The fear of looking foolish to others? Something else?
- Do you think God is embarrassed on your behalf? If not, does that help you feel less embarrassed? Why or why not?

APPLY:
Embarrassment is an unpleasant feeling that makes us wish we could crawl into a hole and disappear. The original meaning of the word had to do with something that bars our way, that impedes us, blocks us, or hinders us from moving forward. When we consider embarrassment in that light, we can see that it's an emotion that can easily hold us back from serving God.

These verses tell us the sort of actions that *should* embarrass us: silly arguments over semantics, empty chatter that does nothing to build up others or ourselves, and lies and deceptions. Our words have power to build or destroy, and this passage of scripture reminds us to use them carefully.

Any other embarrassment we might feel about looking silly in others' eyes is a false sense of shame. God couldn't care less! If we are diligent to please Him and do His work, why should we care what others think of us?

PRAY:
Help me, God, to care less about what others think of me—and more about what You think. Remind me to use my words with care, in Your service.

I FEEL LIKE GIVING UP

READ JOHN 16

KEY VERSE:
*"These things I have spoken to you,
so that in Me you may have peace.
In the world you have tribulation, but take
courage; I have overcome the world."*
JOHN 16:33 NASB

UNDERSTAND:

- What circumstances in your life make you feel like giving up?
- Compare the meanings of "giving up" and "surrendering." Is there a difference? Why does giving up imply failure—and yet God asks us to surrender everything to Him?

APPLY:

Can you imagine how Jesus' followers must have felt when they heard that Jesus planned to leave them? Their hearts must have sank within them—and yet they couldn't have imagined all they would be called to face in the years ahead. Jesus knew there would be times when they would feel like giving up, and He wanted to equip them ahead of time to face the hardships that lay ahead, so that they would not stumble and fall (verse 1).

The same promises Jesus made to His disciples He makes to us today. He assures us that His peace is available to us, even in the midst of all the challenges life brings. "Take courage," He says. "Don't give up. I have already overcome all your problems. Just wait and see what I will do."

PRAY:
Jesus, may I know Your peace today. Give me the courage I need to keep going. I surrender all my fear and anxiety to You—so that You can give me the strength to never give up.

I CAN'T CONTROL MY THOUGHTS

READ ROMANS 8:5–14

KEY VERSE:
Those who are dominated by the sinful nature think about sinful things, but those who are controlled by the Holy Spirit think about things that please the Spirit.
ROMANS 8:5 NLT

UNDERSTAND:

- What sort of thoughts plague you most? Worries? Sexual thoughts? Resentment, jealousy, or envy? Something else? Identifying the thoughts that are disturbing your relationship with God can be the first step toward letting God take them from you.
- What role do you think selfishness plays in your unruly thoughts? Are you truly willing to give them up? Or does some part of you actually enjoy them? Are you secretly holding on to them, reluctant to let them go?

APPLY:
Thoughts can be destructive. We may think that so long as we don't act on our interior thoughts, they will hurt no one. These verses remind us, however, that when we let selfishness and sinfulness control our minds, we are heading down a road that leads toward inner and outer death. God's Spirit of love leads in the opposite direction, toward life and peace (verse 6).

Selfishness does not acknowledge God's right to our lives. It is hostile to His purpose for our lives (verse 7). It seems as though it will bring us the things we want most, but in reality, it takes from us everything that our hearts truly need—the love and companionship of God and others.

We need to pay attention to our thoughts. When we see that they are leading us away from God, we can consciously turn them around. If we clean out all the garbage from our minds, the Spirit will have room to dwell there.

PRAY:
Spirit of God who raised Jesus from the dead, live in me, I pray. Destroy all that is sinful and selfish in me. May my every thought lead me closer to You.

I'M SCARED THAT MY MARRIAGE IS IN TROUBLE

READ 1 PETER 3:8–11

KEY VERSE:
All of you should be of one mind. Sympathize with each other. Love each other as brothers and sisters.
1 PETER 3:8 NLT

UNDERSTAND:

- What makes you worry about the health of your marriage? Is it the way your spouse acts—or is it the way you feel?
- What do you think it means to "be of one mind"? How might you experience that, in practical ways, within your marriage?
- Have you ever thought about loving your spouse as a brother or sister in Christ (even while keeping your sexual relationship intact)? How might that attitude change your marriage?

APPLY:
Almost all marriages go through times of

harmony and happiness, interspersed with times of conflict and pain. Hopefully, the happy times are longer than the painful periods, but no matter how much you love your spouse, it's never going to be easy for two people to live together! Your selfishness will rub against theirs, causing you both pain. You won't always grow, emotionally and spiritually, at the same rate, which means that sometimes one person may feel left behind. The changing circumstances of your lives will bring new challenges to face.

But none of these things needs to threaten the security of your marriage. This passage of scripture gives good advice for building a strong and healthy marriage: don't head in different directions; sympathize with each other; be humble and tenderhearted; don't exchange insults; and finally, search hard for peace—and then do the work that's necessary to maintain it.

PRAY:
God of love, I ask that You bless my marriage. Make it strong. Heal its broken areas. Keep us from hurting one another. Keep us both firmly committed to one another—and to You.

I'M UNSURE WHICH PATH TO TAKE

READ PSALM 25

KEY VERSE:
*Show me your ways, LORD, teach me
your paths. Guide me in your truth and
teach me, for you are God my Savior,
and my hope is in you all day long.*
PSALM 25:4–5 NIV

UNDERSTAND:

- In what areas of your life do you need God's guidance today?
- How do you expect God to show you the path to take? It's unlikely He will send a direct message to you, speaking in an audible voice or writing you a letter. How else might you be able to perceive God's direction? Where should you turn to seek His will for your life?

APPLY:

Again and again, in all the various difficult situations we face, the Bible gives us the same answer: Trust in God. Rely only on Him. Surrender everything into His loving hands. That's the only thing that will put us in the position where God can help us.

God always longs to help. He is waiting for opportunities to demonstrate His love to us. He yearns to show us the path that will lead to our health and healing and happiness. And He will do exactly that. . .if we let Him.

Sometimes, however, even though we may be begging God to show us the path to take, we don't want to hear His answer. Deep inside, we've already chosen the path we'd prefer—and we're afraid God will send us in a different direction. We need to remember that God only wants what's best for us. All His ways are loving and faithful (verse 10).

No matter how many times we rebel against God, choosing to go our own way rather than His, all we have to do is ask His forgiveness. His love and mercy for us are infinite.

PRAY:
Teach me the way You want me to go, God. Guide my path. Lead me closer to You. Guard my life and rescue me; do not let me be put to shame, for I take refuge in You (verse 20).

I'M AFRAID TO TRUST YOU, GOD

READ 1 JOHN 4:13–21

KEY VERSE:
*There is no fear in love. But perfect
love drives out fear, because fear has
to do with punishment. The one who
fears is not made perfect in love.*
1 JOHN 4:18 NIV

UNDERSTAND:

- How are trust and love related?
- Are you afraid of God? If so, do you really believe He loves you, unconditionally, just as you are?
- What connection between the love of God and the love of others does this passage indicate?

APPLY:

The message woven throughout this entire book is this: trust in God is what gives us the courage and strength to face life's difficult times. But what if we're simply too afraid to trust?

To some extent, trust is an act of will, a

moment-by-moment decision to commit everything to God. But God does not want us to have to grit our teeth and screw up our courage every time we come near Him. What He really wants with us is an intimate love relationship. Trust naturally thrives in that state of mutual intimacy.

How can we build that relationship with God, Someone we can neither see nor touch? John tells us the way in verse 17: "In this world we are like Jesus." In other words, if we act as Jesus would, demonstrating love to everyone with whom we come in contact, we will become so confident of God's love that we forget all our fears.

PRAY:
Teach me to trust You more, Lord, by turning me outward, away from my fears, so that I can give to others—and enter into a new relationship with You. Draw me so close to You that there's no more room for fear inside my heart.

I WISH I KNEW FOR SURE YOU LOVE ME, GOD

READ ROMANS 5:6–11

KEY VERSE:
God showed his great love for us by sending Christ to die for us while we were still sinners.
ROMANS 5:8 NLT

UNDERSTAND:

- What experiences in your life have made it difficult for you to believe in the possibility of unconditional love?
- Does your experience of human love limit your ability to understand God's love? How might you come to know God better, so that you can believe more fully in His love?

APPLY:

God asks us to put everything we have and are in His hands. This act of total trust would be nearly impossible if we thought God might drop the things we give Him—or if we suspected He might actually wish to harm us and make us unhappy. But God's love is like no human being's. It wants only our good; there is nothing selfish in it.

Furthermore, it's reciprocal, as these Bible verses tell us. When God asks us to trust Him with our entire life, He has already given us Himself, totally, endlessly, both through Jesus and through the Spirit. We can surrender to Him, knowing we are completely safe and secure. His love will never diminish us or shame us or hurt us. Through Jesus and the Holy Spirit, we can enter a new relationship with God, one that's built on the intimacy of absolutely unconditional love.

PRAY:
Dear God, I may never be able to truly grasp how much You love me—but I thank You anyway. Thank You for sending Your Son into the world. Thank You that through Him, I can experience the life of Your Spirit. Thank You for being my most intimate, most trusted Friend.

YOU MAY ALSO LIKE...

The 5-Minute Prayer Plan

Many Christians yearn for a dynamic prayer life, but we often get stuck in a repetitive routine of prayer. This practical and inspirational guide will give you new ways to approach prayer with 90 focused 5-minute plans for your daily quiet time. These prayer plans explore a variety of life themes great for all ages.

Paperback / 978-1-68322-462-4 / $5.99

Find this and More from Barbour Publishing at Your Favorite Bookstore or at www.barbourbooks.com